BACKGROUND TO CONTEMPORARY GREECE

VOLUME I

BACKGROUND TO

CONTEMPORARY GREECE

edited by
Marion Sarafis
Martin Eve

MERLIN PRESS
LONDON
BARNES & NOBLE BOOKS
SAVAGE, MARYLAND

© The Merlin Press 1990
First published in Great Britain 1990 by The Merlin Press Ltd
10 Malden Road, London NW5

First published in the United States of America 1990 by
BARNES & NOBLE BOOKS
8507 Bollman Place
Savage, Maryland 20763

Library of Congress Cataloging-in-Publication Data
Available from the Library of Congress

British Library Cataloguing in Publication Data
Background to contemporary Greece.
  1. Greece, 1936-
  I. Sarafis, Marion   II. Eve, Martin
  949.507

ISBN 0 85036 393 4
Combined Cloth Edition ISBN 0 85036 392 6

Printed in Great Britain by Whitstable Litho Printers Ltd
Millstrood Road, Whitstable, Kent
Typesetting by Heather Hems
Tower House, Queen Street, Gillingham, Dorset

CONTENTS

Contributors to Volume I

Roderick Beaton has taught Modern Greek language and literature at the universities of Birmingham and London, and is now Koraes Professor of Modern Greek and Byzantine History, Language and Literature at King's College in the University of London. His major publications are: *Folk Poetry of Modern Greece* (Cambridge U.P., 1980); *The Greek Novel, A.D. 1–1985*, editor (Croom Helm, London, 1986); and *The Medieval Greek Romance* (Cambridge U.P., 1989). In addition he has published many articles on late Byzantine and modern Greek literature, as well as on Greek music and oral tradition.

Peter Mackridge, after teaching Modern Greek language and literature at King's College, London, for seven years, is now University Lecturer in Modern Greek at the University of Oxford and a fellow of St Cross College. He has published *The Modern Greek Language* (Oxford 1985), a descriptive analysis of contemporary standard Greek, as well as studies on Modern Greek dialects. In the field of literature he has edited two novels by Kosmas Politis and published *Dionysios Solomos* (Bristol 1989), a study of Greece's 'national poet'. He has also contributed articles on a number of Greek poets and prosewriters of the nineteenth and twentieth centuries.

Jon V. Kofas was Visiting Associate Professor at Loyola University of Chicago and at Marquette University; he is now a Lecturer at the University of Wisconsin/Whitewater and is the author of numerous books and articles, including *Intervention and Underdevelopment: Greece During the Cold War* (University Park: Penn State Press, 1989); *Authoritarianism in Greece: The Metaxas Regime* (New York: East European Monographs/Columbia University Press, 1981); *Financial Relations of Greece and the Great Powers, 1832–1860* (New York: East European Monographs/Columbia University Press, 1981).

Janet Hart is Assistant Professor of Sociology and Political Science at the University of Michigan, Ann Arbor. She is currently completing a book on women's participation in the Greek resistance, based on interviews with members of the key Greek resistance organisations.

Marion Sarafis has an Oxford Classics degree (1936) and pre-war archaeological experience in Greece. She lived in Greece from 1952-7 as the wife of General Stefanos Sarafis, former C.-in-C. of ELAS. She has edited the English edition of his *ELAS* and also the conference proceedings *Greece: From Resistance to Civil War* in English and Greek editions.

CONTENTS

VOLUME II

PREFACE

I am delighted to be given the opportunity of introducing *Background to Contemporary Greece*. In recent years several books of this kind have appeared. One of the best is Y. A. Kourvetaris and Betty A. Dobratz, *A Profile of Modern Greece in Search of Identity* (Oxford 1987). Many such books are in some degree marred either by an excessively nationalistic tone, by a preconceived ideological stance, or by a perception of Greece as merely an element in a global conflict between super-powers. The contributors to the present volume, who come from four different countries, have to my mind attained an admirable combination of empathy and objectivity in their separate studies.

Professor Beaton describes and illustrates the coming of age of Modern Greek literature, which was until the Second World War dominated by imitation of foreign models and by a 'folkloristic' treatment of local themes. Greece has now a voice of its own not only in poetry, but also in the novel.

Dr Mackridge provides a lucid account of the development of a genuine national language and the demise of the Language Question, which, with its deadly political and social overtones, plagued Greek education and Greek public life for more than a century. In fact Greece has succeeded in little more than a generation in doing what it took many other European nations centuries to achieve, and which many Third World countries are still struggling to attain. Both these chapters are of more than purely Greek interest.

Dr J. Kofas, whose *Greece and the Eastern Crisis 1875–1878* was published in 1975 turns his attention to a detailed analysis of the methods and results of American economic aid to Greece in the post-war years 1947–1963. He argues that, however well intentioned, the various aid programmes had not been thought through and were administered in a short-sighted and ideologically prejudiced way. Thus their results were in many respects damaging rather than helpful. There is a lesson here for rich countries and organisations such as the World Bank, which try to direct and control the economy of under-developed countries by throwing money at deep-seated social and economic problems, especially when geopolitical and military considerations determine the scale and form of the aid offered.

Janet Hart surveys the stages in the emancipation of Greek women, emphasising the breaking of age-old social barriers occasioned by participation in the resistance to the occupiers during the Second World War, the subsequent partial repression, and the new and sudden enlargement of horizons after 1974, which was affected both by developments abroad and by the rapid demographic and social changes taking place in Greek society.

Marion Sarafis, in addition to editing the whole volume, contributes an almost exhaustive bibliography of books in English or Greek on the history of Greece from 1936, when Metaxas established his quasi-Fascist dictatorship, until the present day. This chapter supplements Heinz Richter's *Greece and Cyprus since 1920: Bibliography of Contemporary History* (Heidelberg 1984), and will be an indispensable tool for all serious students of Modern Greece.

Christophe Chiclet contributes a translated and supplemented excerpt from his book *Les Communistes grecs dans la guerre* (1987), which perhaps suffers slightly from being extracted from a larger whole. He draws attention to the inept leadership of the Communist Party in the post-war years, which contributed to the initiation and continuation of the civil war. Like almost all Greek politicians of the time, they probably failed to grasp the nature of the relations between the great powers and the overt or tacit understandings between them.

Procopis Papastratis, whose *British Policy towards Greece during the Second World War* appeared in 1984, turns to an earlier period in his masterly survey of the various moves towards the creation of a Balkan Union in the inter-war years. These ranged from a maximalist programme for a Balkan Confederation, which was utopian, to a minimalist programme of a political alliance to guarantee the frontiers of the Balkan countries. It was this latter programme which led to the Balkan Entente Pact of 1934, based on a Greco-Turkish axis. However the rise of Nazi Germany and its economic and political penetration of all the Balkan states soon made any form of Balkan union an unattainable goal. Perhaps the time has come today to dust off the old files and to look once again at means of increasing cooperation between the Balkan countries, which are united not only by the relative underdevelopment which has been their lot in the capitalist era, but also by a common social and cultural heritage, whose roots go back through Ottoman and Byzantine rule to the Roman Empire.

In a remarkable contribution based largely on unpublished sources Pericles Grambas recounts and analyses the debate within the Greek Communist Party during the years of occupation. The wavering and indecisive leadership of the Party contributed to the avoidable clash with British troops in Athens in December 1944, and ultimately to the Civil War and its long and sad aftermath. It is very easy nearly half a century later to point to mistakes and attribute blame. But the situation in Greece was one which neither the Communists nor any other political group in Greece could have foreseen. The leadership, which traditionally saw its power base in the proletariat of Athens and Thessaloniki, found itself in command, though not always able to control, a huge and largely peasant resistance army which dominated much of the country. Should its aim be to use that army for a revolutionary seizure of power when the Germans withdrew, or to seek an alliance with the traditional parties in a government of national unity which would institute long-needed democratic reforms? Enveloped in the fog of war, with unreliable communications — a point not always sufficiently emphasised by Grambas —, mistrusting, and not always without reason, the politicians of the government in exile, uncertain of the attitudes of the other allied powers, sometimes entertaining utopian projects such as peacefully disarming the British troops who entered Greece after the German retreat, these men tried conscientiously to wrestle with a situation for which they were unprepared. If in the end they failed, they were neither knaves nor fools, but honourable men caught up in problems of far more than Greek dimensions.

Anna Collard's densely informative and often deeply moving account of the perception and memory of the civil war in a village in Agrapha, the mountainous and inaccessible heart of Central Greece, is a model of what anthropological techniques can contribute to history. The author's informants were all local people and largely women. For these people, whose forefathers had maintained virtual independence during the centuries of Ottoman rule – and probably for centuries earlier – the civil war meant not only disruption, destruction and persecution. It changed the whole order of things forever.

Robert McDonald's *Pillar and Tinderbox. Greek Press and the Dictatorship* was published in 1982. In his present article he gives a detailed, almost day-by-day, political history of the origin and course of the military dictatorship of 1967–1974, bringing out the murkily sinister ambiguities surrounding many of its stages. Events in Cyprus inevitably have an important place in his story. The United Kingdom emerges in an unexpectedly good light. On 9 August 1974 it offered to reinforce its troops in the island and to put them under United Nations command, a proposal adamantly resisted by the US Secretary of State Henry Kissinger. This chapter provides a useful supplement to the books of Tsoucalas, Woodhouse and others.

Finally Heinz Richter, author of *British Intervention in Greece. From Varkiza to Civil War* (1986), provides a detailed analysis of Greco-Turkish relations since the end of the Second World War. Basic questions which emerge again and again are that of control of the Aegean, taking the form of disputes about extension of territorial waters, ownership of the Continental shelf, and air traffic control, and that of Cyprus. A third potential source of conflict is that of the Turkish minority in Eastern Thrace and the dwindling Greek Community in Istanbul. Much of the diplomatic and legal argumentation may seem niggling and even childish. But it is essential that it go on. A third of Cyprus is still under Turkish military occupation, and within the last few years Greece and Turkey have been on the brink of armed conflict in the Aegean. Perhaps signs of hope can be discerned today.

The rapprochement between the super-powers takes the south-east flank of NATO out of the limelight; a change of leadership in Cyprus has enabled old questions to be re-opened once more; and Turkey's eagerness to join the European Economic Community, as well as her fear of the spread of Islamic fundamentalism, may make her less ready to press issues with Greece. But there are still many obstacles to be overcome. It will need statesmen of the vision and courage of Venizelos and Atatürk to bring the two countries into genuinely friendly relations again. We can only hope that such leaders are waiting in the wings.

This book should be on the reading list of all those interested in Greece, her politics, her economy, her foreign relations and her culture. Every public library in English-speaking countries should make sure that it is on their shelves.

Robert Browning

GREEK LITERATURE SINCE NATIONAL
INDEPENDENCE – A CONSPECTUS

Roderick Beaton

Literary history, and the literary history of Greece is no exception, is traditionally a matter of names and dates. Anyone with a special interest in the country will have encountered the name of Solomós, Palamás, Cavafy, Seféris, Elytis among poets, of Kazantzákis – and who else? – among novelists. And even of some of these, very little of the work is available in English translation. My aim in this essay is to keep names and dates to a minimum, although in the nature of things they cannot be excluded altogether. Rather my hope is to place the more familiar names in a context of historical and literary movements, rather than merely of other names. And having filled out that context, necessarily only schematically, in the first part of the essay (the historical outline of Greek literature since 1821), I shall proceed to identify particular sources for literary trends in Greece, and suggest ways of exploring this rich and little-known vein of European literature thematically, through characteristic and recurrent themes and approaches to them in the corpus of texts.

1. Historical outline

Although Greek has the longest history of continuous development of any European language, Greek cultural life – and this includes literature – from ancient times until the present can best be regarded as a series of discontinuities. The most recent of these, and in many respects the most radical, occurred in the wake of the declaration of national

1

independence in 1821, and it is from that date that Modern Greek literature, in the restricted sense of the literature of a modern European nation, can be said to begin. Greeks before 1821 had never been part of a nation, and the growth of a modern literature after 1821 is part of the broader attempt of Greek-speakers, emerging from the historical experience of Ottoman domination, to create an identity and establish a tradition of their own which would simultaneously conform to western models and yet be distinctively and uniquely Greek. The history of Greek literature since independence is therefore inseparable from the history of the emergent cultural life of the new nation-state.

In 1821 there were two quite separate centres for learning and intellectual speculation in the Greek-speaking world. One was grouped around the Ecumenical Patriarchate in Constantinople (which had acquired secular power and privileges as it became responsible to the Sultan for the Christian subjects of the Ottoman Empire). Within this sphere intellectual activities were centred on Constantinople and the Danubian principalities of Wallachia and Moldavia, which throughout the 18th century had been governed on behalf of the Ottomans by powerful Greek families close to the Patriarchate. The other was at the opposite end, geographically, of the Greek-speaking world, in the Ionian Islands and principally in their capital, Corfu. These islands had belonged to Venice since late medieval times, and had a large hereditary aristocracy whose sons were traditionally educated at Italian universities. Through these two very different centres the intellectual ideas of Europe in the 18th century came to be echoed and discussed in Greek, and the foundations laid for the cultural development of the new state throughout much of the succeeding century.[1]

Among the Phanariots, as the intellectuals surrounding the Patriarchate (in *Fanári* district of Constantinople) were called, the predominant influence from the west came from France, and the first short stories to be written in Greek were a translation, by Rígas Velestinlís (1757–98) from Rétif de le Bretonne. In poetry too, the 'Bacchic' and 'Erotic' ditties of Athanásios Hristópoulos, who spent most of his life in Jassy, in the Danubian principality of Moldavia, owe much to the inoffensive and stylised naivety of French neo-classicism. It was in the Ionian Islands that the ideas of German

2

Romanticism first found a home among Greek-speakers, in the writings of Dionísios Solomós (1797–1857), who established himself unchallenged as the 'national poet' of the Greeks with the publication of his rousing 'Hymn to Liberty', simultaneously in several languages, in 1825.

Until 1864 the Ionian Islands remained, as they had become after the Napoleonic Wars, a British Protectorate, and for much of the 19th century the separation between the 'School', as it is sometimes called, of these islands and the cultural life of Athens, the new national capital, remained evident. Athens, upon its foundation as a new national capital in 1834, was in the most literal sense a cultural vacuum. Into this vacuum came Phanariots from Constantinople and the Danubian principalities: the brothers Panayiótis and Aléxandros Soútsos, and the poet and later novelist Aléxandros Rízos Rangavís. The first introduced Romantic poetry and the epistolary novel to Greece, the second political satire and the third the historical novel which became the dominant form of prose literature until the 1880s. (The work of all three, but especially the Romantic historical novel as introduced by Rangavís, is lampooned in the most sophisticated Athenian novel of the period, *Pope Joan* by Emmanouíl Roídis [1866][2].)

New departures in drama written for the stage are made early on, and quite independently, both in the Ionian Islands and in Athens. Andónios Mátesis' *The Basil Plant*, in which the values of the old aristocracy of the islands are pitted against the new ideas of the French Enlightenment, was written for performance in Zákinthos in 1830; in Athens, Dimítrios Hatzí-Aslán, a Phanariot who had renamed himself Vizándios ('of Byzantium') on arrival in independent Greece, wrote the first version of his stage-play *Babel* in 1836. The wittiest contribution to the long-running 'Language Question' ever made, this play presents a group of Greeks from different regions gathered in a Náfplion *taverna* to celebrate the victory at Navarino. Their inability to understand one another's dialect leads to violence and they all end up celebrating their newfound liberty in jail. After these two promising starts, however, Greek drama quickly becomes the poor relation to poetry and prose fiction that it remains today.

The two 'schools' begin to approach one another in the work of Aristotélis Valaorítis (1824–79) from Lefkás in the

3

Ionian Islands, who became one of the first deputies to represent the islands in the Greek Parliament on their cession to Greece in 1864. Valaorítis' verse uses the traditional verseforms and the spoken language favoured at the time in his native islands but not in Athens, but the subject matter of his most ambitious works — verse dramas on heroic martyrdoms in Greek history — places him alongside the historical and nationalist preoccupations of Athenian writers of his time. The distinctive heritage of the Ionian Islands then becomes progressively merged with that of Athens, which by the end of the century has in any case outgrown its origins in the Patriarchate of Constantinople.

After about 1880 a new direction is given to both poetry and prose by the (surprisingly belated) discovery of oral folklore as a means of establishing national identity and also as a source for the raw materials of literature. Poets such as Yeóryios Drosínis (1859–1951) and Kóstas Kristállis (1868–1894) begin publishing poems in which the styles and rural preoccupations of oral folk poetry were reflected, and in 1883 the announcement in the influential periodical *Estía* of a competition for a 'short story on a Greek theme' initiated a decisive turn away from the historical and the heroic to a new kind of literary realism which took its subjects from life in remote villages of the Greek mountains and islands. This movement produced two writers of novels and short stories of European stature — Aléxandros Papadiamándis (1851–1911)[3] and Andréas Karkavítsas (1864–1922).[4] The innovative and disturbingly modern short stories of Yeóryios Viziinós (1849–1896) published between 1883 and 1895 also owe something to this movement.[5]

The colossus of modern Greek poetry, Kostís Palamás (1859–1943), bestrides the turn of the century. Palamás shared his contemporaries' interest in folk poetry, but unlike them went further to achieve a grandiose synthesis, in which the native Greek oral tradition plays its part alongside European late Romanticism, Symbolism and the ideas of Wagner and Nietzsche.[6]

Greek literature in the 20th century is less easy to categorise chronologically. The first writers to be mentioned published their work well into the century, but have a much closer relation to what had gone before in the 19th century than to most of their contemporaries. These deserve to be called, after W. B. Yeats, the 'last Romantics': Níkos Kazantazákis (1883–1957), 'Angelos Sikelianós (1884–1951) and Kóstas Várnalis (1884–1974). Kazantzákis, the failed dramatist and dubiously received epic poet, turned his hand in 1941 to the first of seven novels that would gain him an international reputation unmatched by any other Greek novelist. But his grandiose themes, his interweaving of philosophical speculation with literature, and the forms in which he preferred to write (traditional metres in poetry, rural realism in the novel) place him in the company of his 19th-century predecessors.[7] The same can be said for another visionary on the grand scale, Sikelianós, who from his first long, exultant poem published in 1909 (and called 'The Visionary') to his more measured and shorter poems of the 1930s and '40s, sought to give renewed life to the myths and traditions of Greece through the ages by sheer force of literary rhetoric.[8] Várnalis, after a dramatic conversion to Marxism in 1919 which cost him his professional career as a schoolteacher, made brilliant use of the equivocal dramatic monologue as it had been perfected by Browning in England in the previous century. In the mixed prose and verse of *The Light that Burns* (1922), the poems of *Slaves Besieged* (1927) and the quirky prose text, *The True Apology of Socrates* (1933) he gives a new direction to traditional literary forms and 'philosophical' satire, but refused ever to abandon traditional forms of verse or to question the nature of literature itself. All three writers share a particularly 19th-century conception of literature as a vehicle for propounding philosophical or quasi-philosophical ideas.

Despite their close engagement with contemporary issues, Kazantzakis, Sikelianós and Várnalis represent a powerful conservative force in 20th-century Greek literature, both in the forms they considered appropriate to literary expression, and in the way in which they implicitly saw literature as functioning. Modernism, the literary movement which in western Europe reached its full development in the early '20s as a reaction against precisely these assumptions of the late 19th century, appears more modestly in Greece, and not clearly until the decade of the '30s. In its broadest sense, Modernism includes all types of writing which question the nature of the literary text, the communicability or the objective validity of private experience, and the relation of literature, as language, to the outside world. This broad sense, applied to Greek literature, would embrace the subtle ironies and probings of the historical and sexual 'underside' of things in the poems published in Alexandria by Constantine Cavafy (Kaváfis) between 1904 and his death in 1933.[9] It would also extend to cover the self-destructive wit and morbid longing for oblivion of Kóstas Kariotákis, whose suicide in 1928 at the age of thirty-two came as the tragic culmination of a rhetorical strategy which had sought fulfilment in its own extinction.

But Modernism proper, more narrowly defined as a literary movement sharing well-defined aims, begins in Greece in the 1930s. In prose its first and most uncompromising appearance is made in the provinces: in the novels and short stories of Stélios Xefloúdas, Alkiviádis Yiannópoulos, Níkos Gavriíl Pentzíkis in Thessaloníki, and the maverick Beckettian *avant la lettre*, Yiánnis Skarímbas in Halkída. In the capital, however, although new ideas about the novel are apparent in the first novels of George Theotokás (*Argo* 1933–6) and Pandelís Prevelákis (*The Tale of a Town*, 1938), only Kosmás Polítis, in his three novels published during the '30s, makes a significant break with realism. The novels of this and the following decades which are still the most read, however, hark back to the rural realism of the late 19th century, and beyond it to the techniques and mythical world of native Greek oral traditions: they are *Life in the Tomb* by Strátis Mirivílis (1930)[10] and *Aeolian Earth* (1943) by Ilías Venézis.[11]

Modernism in verse makes a fairly spectacular appearance in the annus mirabilis, 1935. As well as the first edition in Greece of Cavafy's collected poems, that year saw the publication of George Seféris' third book, entitled *Mithistórima* or *Novel*, a collection of twenty-four brief poems indebted for their style and technique to aspects of Eliot's *The Waste Land* and Joyce's *Ulysses;*[12] of *Blast Furnace*, an uncompromising series of brief prose-poems by Greece's first fully-fledged Surrealist writer, Andréas Embiríkos; and the first appearance in print of early poems by Odysseus Elytis who, like Seféris was later to become a Nobel prize-winner.[13] The prolific Yiánnis Rítsos, whose first book was published in 1934, quickly began to distance himself from the resolution of the Communist Writers'

Congress in Moscow in that year, which had called for an end to formal experiments in literature, and forged a distinctive path of his own in which the modernist techniques and stylistic experiments of his non-Marxist contemporaries, allied to an unwavering ideological commitment, have produced a precarious synthesis of peculiar richness and complexity.[14]

Perhaps because of prose fiction's natural affinity to historical writing (see below), the purely Modernist phase of the Greek novel was relatively short-lived. Fiction from World War II until 1974 was much more referential and less preoccupied with questions of form and the nature of the medium than it had been in the '30s. Not so poetry, however, which has continued a linear development since the mid-30s. Post-war poems by Seféris and Elytis make frequent allusions to the traumatic events of the Albanian campaign and the Occupation, but reference to the Civil War, when it occurs at all, is cryptic, almost shamefaced. Seféris in a poem of 1946, ' "Thrush" ', refers to the sons of Oedipus, Eteokles and Polyneikes — brothers who fought to the death — and Elytis in his 1959 masterpiece, *To 'Axion Estí*, tells an obscure parable about a sheepfold in which 'my people themselves are the door and my people themselves are the sheepfold and the flock of sheep'. On the other hand Rítsos in one of his most famous poems, 'Romiosíni', which dates from that period, portrays the Civil War as a war waged by Greece's enemies against the very land, and the younger generation of poets who began to publish during the '40s, notably Míltos Sahtoúris and Tákis Sinópoulos, reflect the experiences of their formative years in an imagery of obsessive violence.[15] Rítsos by the '60s had learnt from Seféris, and many of his most effective poems from that decade often subvert for their own purposes Seféris' technique of referring to the ancient or mythical Greek past as a point of departure, often combined to striking effect with imagery of seemingly free association derived from Surrealism.

It is obviously too soon, writing in 1988, to make any historical assessment of the so-called 'generation of the '70s' which emerged out of the junta years (1967–74) and whose momentum continues unabated. In poetry the dominant presences behind the work of Leftéris Poúlios, Jenny Mastoráki, Násos Vayenás, Yiánnis Kondós among many

7

others remain, in varying proportions, those of Seféris and of Surrealism. In prose, after the relatively realistic achievements of the '60s (Stratís Tsírkas' trilogy, *Drifting Cities,*[16] set in the Middle East during World War II, and Kóstas Taktsís' comic tour de force, still unrivalled, *The Third Wedding*[17]), have given way to the greater confidence and unpretentious competence of such novels, very different from one another, as *The Box* by ´Aris Alexándrou (1974), *Fool's Gold (I Arhéa Skouriá)* by Máro Doúka (1979) and *Istoría* by Yióryis Yiatromanolákis (1982). In all three novels the politics of the left play an important part, and are dissected, although from a sympathetic position, with biting irony. In all three, indigenous styles of story-telling, particularly in the use of indirect speech and the unbroken monologue of a single narrator, are combined with elements drawn from the tradition of rural realism that goes back, via the late 1930s and '40s to the 1880s, together with a renewed Modernist questioning of literary conventions. Doúka's novel is much more realistic than the other two, but even here dreams and fantasies interrupt the presentation of real events, and the temporal sequence of the story is cunningly distorted. *Fool's Gold* could be described as the novel of the generation who were students during the Colonels' regime; *The Box* is a bitter allegory of the failure of Communism in the Civil War, presented as the failure to break out of inflexible and out-moded linguistic codes, and ends by representing the failure of language itself ever to signify: the box for which the soldiers on an urgent secret mission have sacrificed their lives turns out to be empty. *Istoría* returns to the rural setting of the novels and short stories of the late 19th century but with a difference, as the banal events of a vengeance killing in Crete at the time of Venizelos are woven into a discourse which consciously imitates that of the first historian, Herodotos.

2. The sources of Modern Greek literature

No literary tradition exists in a vacuum. So far I have tried to sketch the interrelations between Greek literature and the history and cultural life of Greeks during the last two centuries. But Greek literature, like any other literary tradition, is also a response to purely literary events, that is, to the existence of other texts, and the cultural prestige attributed to other traditions, more or less remote either in time or in space. By 'sources' in this section I mean those literary traditions, either not modern or not Greek, which have played a formative role in shaping the course of modern Greek literature since national independence. These are: ancient Greek literature; writing in a form of the spoken language produced in the late Middle Ages and under the influence of the Renaissance; Greek oral traditions, whether in poetry or prose; and finally the literary movements of western Europe since the late 18th century.

An essential component of the national identity of the new state in the 19th century was the claim to racial descent from the ancient Hellenes. Much of the debate about the form of language appropriate for public life and literature begins from the assumption that the glories of the classical past are more or less literally to be revived. The existence of a classical tradition too hallowed for the modern writer even to attempt to surpass, and too remote to be seriously imitated has burdened the modern Greek writer with a highly ambiguous asset. The classical inheritance is a matter for pride, but it is also, as George Savidis has put it, an intolerable burden.[18] One problem has been that classical literature in the last two centuries has had to be painfully re-acquired by Greeks who were largely excluded from its revival in the west during the Renaissance, and cannot easily be re-appropriated in any other way than through the editions, commentaries and scholarship of western Europeans. In practice, the literature of classical antiquity became not so much a *source* for the modern literary tradition as one of its abiding *themes*. Poets from Solomós to Elytis and novelists as different as Papadiamándis at the end of the 19th century and Tsírkas in the mid-20th, have striven in their work to recuperate something of the ancient tradition for the modern world, and poignantly report the near-impossibility of doing so.

A predecessor of Greek literature after 1821 much less remote, though still at a remove, is afforded by the experiments in vernacular literature dating from the last years of the Byzantine empire, and more particularly by the sophisticated literary tradition which flourished in Crete under Venetian rule from the 14th to the 17th centuries. The 10,000-line verse romance *Erotókritos,*[19] written in Venetian Crete in the early 17th century and the Senecan tragedy *Erofíli* by Hortátsis from the same period circulated in cheap printed editions during the Ottoman centuries, and older manuscripts had been preserved in the Ionian Islands, to which many educated Cretans had fled after the Ottoman conquest of 1669. Something of the language of these texts — a vigorous literary idiom based on the Cretan dialect — and the metrical form in which they are written, were rehabilitated by the 'national poet' and first Greek Romantic, Solomós, in his self-appointed task of creating a new literary language and style for the nation, and Solomós pays tribute to the Cretan substratum of his own writing in his narrative poem about a Cretan refugee from Turkish atrocities in his native island, 'The Cretan' (1833).[20] Earlier literature in vernacular Greek, the romances of love and marvels composed in the 14th and 15th centuries, and the even older *chanson de geste, Diyenís Akrítis*, whose action is set on the remote frontiers of Byzantium in eastern Anatolia before the 12th century, were rediscovered later in the century, and exercised an evident influence upon Palamás. Diyenís in particular, as the hero of contemporary oral folk songs as well as of a medieval epic poem, caught the literary imagination at the end of the century, and has often since figured in literature as the representative of ideal Greek heroism.

The case of Diyenís leads us naturally to the third tradition on which modern Greek writers have been able to draw: that of oral tradition and particularly of oral folk songs. It was Solomós, once again, who first recognised the importance for a nation which had no real *literary* tradition, of this form of verbal art — 'these traces' as Solomós called them. These unwritten traditions have an impenetrably long history behind them, and present to the would-be modern poet an example of his own language already highly stylised for formal narrative and lyrical utterance. While Solomós was right to frown on his successors whom he accused of merely imitating the style of folk songs, there is no doubt that the diction, metrical form and even something of the worldview of his own late poems represent a meeting point of traditional oral poetry with the dominant European discourse of Romanticism. At least up until Seféris the world of folk poetry has also provided a fixed reference point, comparable to that afforded in English by Shakespeare or the King James Bible, to which allusions of all sorts can be made in the confident knowledge that they will be recognised by Greek readers. In this spirit Sikelianós could entitle a highly abstract verse drama *The Death of Diyenís*, Kazantzákis in an early play and Eyltis in *To 'Axion Estí* could make metaphorical use of the story of the master-builder's wife immured into the foundations of a bridge to make it stand firm, from the folk song 'The Bridge of Arta', and Rítsos could present the lament of a mother whose son had been shot down in a workers' demonstration with a title (*'Epitáfios'*) and formal characteristics which point to the oral 'Lament of the Virgin' still sung in villages as part of the Easter ritual, and through it to a (much transformed) 'resurrection'.

These are the three native substrata on which modern Greek literature is founded, and it is its unique relation to these earlier traditions, as well as to contemporary Greek history, that determines to a large extent the specific character of Greek literature since the early 19th century. The influence of European movements is, superficially at least, more evident than that of any native Greek tradition, and it is certainly in response to European developments that most of the main historical lines of development outlined in the previous section have taken place. Thus the first poetry of the nation is the Romantic poetry of Solomós, influenced (although through intermediaries) by Hegel, Schiller and Byron, perhaps also by Goethe and Wordsworth; the first novels were historical novels whose debt to Walter Scott is immediately apparent. Even the rural realism in prose at the end of the 19th century, which is often thought of as a peculiarly Greek phenomenon, is contemporary with the Wessex novels of Hardy, the Sicilian novels of Giovanni Verga, the vignettes of Normandy life by Flaubert and Maupassant. The process is still more evident in the 20th century. Greek Modernism gains the ascendant in the 1930s, a decade later than in western Europe; realism returns, in prose at least, in the '50s and '60s, again a decade later than in the west. Among individual writers Kazantzákis loudly proclaimed his indifference to Greek literature and all the

11

mentors that he acknowledged (at least) are either non-Greek or non-literary; Seféris' enormously influential poetics are part of a conscious response to the poetics of Eliot and Joyce; Cavafy was an assiduous reader of the English Victorians and began his career by trying to imitate them; Theotokás in 1929 roundly condemned the provincialism of Greek rural realism and in his novel of 1933–6 (*Argo*) seeks to emulate Dostoyevsky and Gide.

The list is endless; indeed the impression is easily gained that each generation in Greek literature represents a new start, in which the work of predecessors is decisively rejected in favour of whatever has recently been happening in the west. Certainly modern Greek literature has declared itself an integral part of the European tradition, and to that extent the intertextual references and allusions by which all literary works make themselves intelligible at all must be to that tradition. But it is probably mistaken to see this relationship as one of abject dependence. Theotokás put this problem well in 1929 when he wrote that, 'The trouble with Modern Greek literature is not that it has taken a great deal, but that it has given nothing in return.' There are signs that this situation is at last changing. But even when we look at what Greek writers have 'taken', the process may well turn out to be less derivative than it looks at first sight. Are the true masters of Kazantzákis really Christ, Buddha, Lenin and a workman called George Zorbás, as he declared? Are his true literary precursors really Homer, Dante and Goethe (all of whom he translated)? Or are his novels not rather more the heirs of the rural realism (which conceals an ambiguous critique of Nietzsche), that he could have read in Karkavítsas' *The Beggar* (1896) and in Mirivílis' *Life in the Tomb* and *Vasilis Arvanitis* (1934–43)[21]? To what extent do Seféris' posthumously published diaries and unfinished novel of the '20s reveal his poetics already well developed before ever he came into contact with Eliot and Joyce? And what are we to make of those more enigmatic figures of the Greek literary stage — Sikelianós or Rítsos — who seem never to have read anything at all?

3. Themes and modes of representation

By way of a corrective to the preceding section, which by its nature tended to minimise the specificity of modern Greek literature, I should like now to isolate a number of specific themes and modes of representation which recur with sufficient prominence in Greek literature to be regarded as characteristic of it. This is not to claim that any of the subjects touched on in this section is *peculiar* to Greek literature. In literary studies anywhere there is very little 'new under the sun', and all of the points I shall be making here naturally invite comparison with other literary traditions. I have chosen these themes only because the relative frequency with which they appear in Greek literature in our period seems to me (subjectively of course) striking and therefore worthy of some discussion. It is not accidental that all of them can be traced back to the first 'national' poet, Dionísios Solomós, and I shall illustrate each of them first with reference to that writer. *

Contemporary history ('Testimonies'). Solomós first gained the attention of his fellow-Greeks and of a wide international public among the philhellenes of Europe and America with the publication, as has already been mentioned, of his topical 'Hymn of Liberty' in 1825. Although his own poetics quickly outgrew the unabashedly bloodthirsty nationalism of this poem and of its companion piece, a swashbuckling 'Ode upon the Death of Lord Byron', it is this far more than the subtly exploratory Romantic fragments which followed, that has assured his reputation among readers up until the present day, and has surely helped to guide later poets and even prose writers towards their engagement with the less widely-known poems of Solomós' maturity. Even in his later years Solomós never abandoned his allegiance to contemporary history, although his interests had by now gone far beyond the political and nationalistic. His poem 'The Cretan' (1833) refers, superficially at least, to the Cretan rising that coincided with the declaration of national independence in the Peloponnese in 1821; the successive drafts of an 'epic' poem, *The Free Besieged* (1826–49), owe their ostensible subject matter to events in Mesolonghi in 1826; and the late poem 'The Shark' (1849) again takes a topical event as its starting point, although the death of a young English soldier attacked by a shark while bathing, is an event of a very different order from the historical subjects of his earlier poems. This allegiance to the world of events, and especially events of

13

significance to the nation, is noteworthy in Solomós because in literary terms it seems superfluous in his later work; indeed the determination that 'The Free Besieged' would be the epic of the fall of Mesolonghi is so much at odds with the fragmentary sections of the poem that Solomós actually wrote, that one could easily suppose that it was this allegiance that prevented him from finishing any of his later works to his own satisfaction.

But Solomós' instinct that literature has a duty ('The Free Besieged' was originally to have been entitled *To Hréos* — 'Duty') to bear witness to contemporary history has found strong echoes in later generations. In the novels of the mid-19th century the recent history of the War of Independence plays a prominent part; in the 20th century the most widely read novels remain the factually presented, 'I-was-there' novels of Mirivílis about the First World War, of Venézis and Doúkas about the Asia Minor Catastrophe; and post-war fiction, as well as a good deal of poetry, up until the early '70s dealt in a representational way with the traumatic events of the 1940s. In the same way many of Seféris' poems contain implicit commentary on contemporary political and historical events; Elytis' *To 'Axion Estí* is at one level a metaphorical chronicle of the German Occupation, and two collections of short poems that Rítsos wrote during the 1960s have the title *Martiríes* (Testimonies). All of this literary writing pays implicit homage to the oral or popular history of the testimony or chronicle. The importance of the former in a society which is largely non-literate (as Greek society was until the early part of this century) is easy to understand. And the popular chronicle as a means of disseminating information, and also as a literary form, has a continuous history going back to early Byzantine times. Literature, in Greece, still preserves a respect and even envy for direct oral discourse, and is reluctant to renounce its function, as an auxiliary to historiography, in communicating the essence of actual events.

Historical realism. This is really only an extension of the previous theme backwards beyond the reach of direct oral testimony, but it tends to confirm the impression that for many Greek writers and readers historical 'truth' is by nature superior to literary 'imagining'. In Solomós as in many later writers there is an overlap between contemporary testimony and past history: by the time he was writing his fragmentary drafts of the 1830s and '40s the events of the War of Independence had already become part of history, and while the 'Hymn of Liberty' was a cry of the moment, the second and third versions of 'The Free Besieged' can be seen rather as the attempt to comprehend the events of that same period now from the perspective of history. Remoter history was also not unknown to Solomós – his poem 'The Cretan' implies a link between the contemporary revolt in Crete and the struggles that had taken place in the island almost two hundred years before, when the literary and artistic Renaissance of the island under Venetian rule had come to an abrupt end. He even worked for a time on a poem about Nikifóros Vriénnios, a Byzantine rebel of the late 11th century, based (via Schiller) on the *Alexiad* of Anna Komniní.

When prose fiction later became established in Athens it was the historical novel, with the nationalist overtones it had acquired from Walter Scott, that became the most popular form. Rangavís in 1850 published *The Lord of Morea*, like Solomós' unfinished poem derived from a historical work of the Byzantine period, and Roḯdis savagely parodied the genre in his *Pope Joan* (1866). Even Mátesis' play about contemporary social conflict in Zákinthos, which for tactical reasons only he had set more than a century in the past, when it came to be published in Athens thirty years after it had been written, had to be described by its author as 'a historical novel dramatically represented'. Even after the vogue for the historical novel was over, the attempt of literature to recover the historical past continued – in the 'epic'-style poems of Palamás set in Byzantine times, in the possibly allegorical recourse to the distant past by novelists in the time of Metaxás and under the German Occupation, in the title and Herodotean pretensions of Yiatromanolákis' novel, *Istoría*, of 1982 – and above all, of course, in the historical poems of Cavafy which represent one of the most penetrating and disturbing explorations ever made of the relation between the power of events and the power of writing to shape what we think of as 'history'.

The surreal imagination. This cannot be called a theme, but is rather a characteristic of the way in which any theme, often those just mentioned which are closely bound to the world of real events, may be represented in literature. My

15

example from Solomós is chosen almost at random:

> So reigned the thunder,
> And the sea, that raged like boiling broth,
> Was quieted; all calm and polished clean,
> Fragrant as flowers, it mirrored all the stars . . .
> But close by the Girl, who gladly clung to me,
> The full moon trembled limpid on the water.
> At once unfolds a wonder, and from that spot
> Issues before me One all clad in the moon.
> The cool light shivered at the godlike vision,
> Her eyes' black depths and hair of gold.
> She gazed on the stars and they exulted
> Growing brighter, not hiding her from sight.
> Without a wrinkle on the sea she rose,
> A cypress insubstantial all her height . . .

(The Cretan)

Critics are still undecided about what this vision 'represents'. What is clear is that what is being described is an imaginative experience far removed from the world of objective, verifiable fact. The vision is constructed out of a series of associations — the opposition between a stormy sea and absolute calm, between the nighttime setting and the 'light of noon' that a few lines on will spread about the apparition, but most important between the world of nature and the inner state of mind of the human subject. Other associations progress by means of likeness: the calm suggests the fragrance of flowers, the mirror to which the sea is compared and out of which the apparition rises; the figurative clothing of the female figure 'all clad in the moon' follows from the natural appearance of the moon reflected on the water; her slender figure evokes in turn the traditional symbol (in the folk tradition) of the cypress tree, with its ambivalent connotations of youthful suppleness and of death. The series of associations enables the poet to project the incommunicable inner state of mind of his narrator upon nature as a kind of mirror. The result is far from natural; rather the elements or images which belong to nature are distorted out of their normal context, subjected to the controlling force of the human imagination and the discourse in which they are inscribed. It is begging many questions to describe such a use of imagery as 'surreal'; what is significant here, as in the modes of writing which later tried to capture in language *surréalité*, is that images and the ideas they connote are linked by a non-rational process of association.

Imagery recognisably of this type recurs throughout modern Greek literature, often in the most unlikely contexts, and can be traced back to folk poetry where the technique of non-logical association is highly developed.[22] It is prominent in the 'rural realist' short stories of Papadiamándis; in his contemporary Viziinós not so much in the form of imagery as in the organisation of his short-stories, all of which involve the equivalent of *trompe l' oeil* effects; in Palamás and all the major 20th-century poets, but surprisingly often in prose fiction as well. Instead of further enumeration I offer two brief illustrations, the first a short poem of Rítsos written in 1968, the second an extract from ´Aris Alexándrou's allegory, in novel form, of the Greek Civil War, published in 1974:

SIGNS

Afterwards the statues were overgrown entirely by weeds. We didn't
    know
whether the statues got smaller or the weeds got higher.
    Only
a great bronze hand was visible above the undergrowth
in the shape of a misplaced, terrible blessing. The woodcutters
went by on the lower road — not turning their heads at all.
The women didn't sleep with their husbands. Nights
we could hear the apples falling one by one into the river;
    and then
the stars peacefully sawing away at that bronze, raised hand.

(Y. Rítsos, Stones, Repetitions, Barbed Wire)

In Alexándrou's novel the narrator pays a nocturnal visit, unannounced, to the village where a girlfriend lives whom he hasn't seen for several years:

. . . I saw Réna standing in her long white nightgown (she must have got up out of bed and been standing there watching me without uttering a word or crying out . . . motionless, I couldn't see her face clearly, although the moon was just then rising and the two large windows of the corner room were uncurtained) there was Réna standing and I took a step towards her, and another and another, closer to her whispering, 'It's me' and then she raised her right hand and at first it seemed to me that she was giving me her hand, to shake it formally (if such a thing were possible!) but no, she raised it high up, as though to repulse me, I saw the palm turned towards me, but still not uttering a word out of her mouth and I didn't want to alarm her, I set aside the hand . . . I embraced her and at that moment . . . [there follows a climactic parenthesis of 13 lines]

... at that moment I understood that Réna's left arm was missing, the sleeve of her nightgown was empty, the arm cut off a little below the shoulder and I don't know what came over me, I don't know what happened exactly, I must have grabbed her nightgown with both my hands ... and I don't know if I wanted her naked body at that moment, or if I wanted to see her truncated arm, anyhow I stripped Réna naked ... and turned to look at her quite naked as she stood before me, white all over in the light of the moon ... like a gypsum [copy of a] statue ...

(A. Alexándrou, *The Box*, pp. 264–5)

Tradition and national identity

A very different kind of preoccupation of Modern Greek writers at all periods has been with the need to establish a tradition, and in particular to reclaim the achievements of earlier periods of Hellenism in such a way as to give validation to present endeavours. This early poem by Solomós has the title, 'The Shade of Homer':

> A dainty moon shone palely – peace
> Overall, all nature at a standstill,
> And from his lonesome bed
> The nightingale began his plaint;
> From all around the stillness of the night
> Re-echoed that most sweet lament;
> A sleep profound took hold of me at last,
> And lo, before me an old man appeared.
>
> Upon the shore the old man sat;
> About his old, torn clothes
> Sweetly sweetly the blowing of the wind
> wisped his sparse white hair,
> And he towards the starry heavens
> Kept darting his extinguished eyes;
> Slowly slowly he arose,
> And like one with sight came close to me.

In this poem by Solomós, published posthumously as a 'fragment', Homer is in no sense the poet's source. Homer, the oldest representative of the ancient tradition, is rather what the poem is *about*. The modern poet feels his ancient predecessor as a ghostly presence behind him – and a century later Ángelos Sikelianós will describe an encounter with the ancient bard, again on an Ionian seashore, in which the

18

twenty-year old modern will even presume to lead the blind Homer by the hand. Tradition, not in the sense of sources actually underlying modern texts, but rather as the object of reference of these texts, is one of the most commonly recurring themes of modern Greek literature. Frequently, as in the poem of Solomós quoted, it takes the form of a quest for tradition, of a looking back into the past for links that will validate the present. And this whole literary quest is part of the larger quest by Greeks for a national identity in the last two centuries, that was mentioned at the beginning of this essay.

One way of establishing such an identity through literature is of course to write about specifically Greek things — be it contemporary or remoter history or the customs and way of life of rural communities. (It is certainly significant that the urban novel is almost entirely absent until the first decade of the 20th century — the manners of Greek urban society in the 19th century were modelled closely on those of western Europe, and so lacked — or were felt to lack — the essential 'Greekness' of either a heroic past or a ruggedly rural present.) More interesting from our point of view is the frequency with which the search for native traditions becomes a theme of both poetry and prose fiction.

The third novel of Andréas Karkavitsas, *The Archaeologist* (1904), allegorizes this quest in the form of a pseudo-folktale: the Evmorfópoulos ('Beautiful) family, having lost most of its lands and fallen on hard times, is divided as to which course of action to pursue to restore its fortunes now that the predatory landowner (representing the Ottoman Empire) is at a disadvantage. One brother immerses himself in the stuffy books left behind by their ancestors in happier days, and brings in pedantic, monocled foreigners to help him dig up the vegetable patch for statues of long-forgotten Evmorfópouli. He even tries to speak in the obsolete idiom of his dusty books. The younger, more spontaneous brother prefers nature to books and aggressive action to archaeology — and of course champions the living spoken language of their village. The archaeologist brother is finally crushed to death by the weight of one of his ancient statues when he tries to move it. The point of this rather obvious allegory is clear: the ancient heritage is as likely to prove a fatal burden as a trump card in negotiating the revived status of the family of the Greeks.

More interesting than this novel itself is the fact that almost exactly the same image was used by Seféris in the sequence of poems, published in 1935, that established him as the foremost of the modernist 'generation of the '30s', entitled *Novel (Mithistórima)*. Seféris' technique is much surer than that of Karkavítsas with his laboured allegory, and in a few lines Seféris makes telling use of the same symbol of the stature as a 'something incompatible with life':

I awoke with this marble head in my hands
that exhausts my elbows and I don't know where to put it down.
It was falling into the dream as I was emerging from the dream
in this way our lives have been made one and it will be very difficult
    to separate them again.

I look at the eyes; neither open nor closed
I speak to the mouth that ever strives to speak
I hold the cheeks that have passed through the skin.
I have no more strength;

my hands disappear and come close to me
truncated.

Indeed the whole of Seféris poem-sequence from which this short poem is taken deals with the search for a tradition and the need to establish a continuity between the achievements of the dead and the aspirations of the living.

Such a painful acceptance that the ancient tradition could neither be fully recuperated nor ignored had earlier been put in moving terms by Palamás in his long poem, *The twelve cantos of the gipsy* (1907). The hero-narrator of this poem, the gipsy of the title, has neither home nor history nor tradition. For all three he substitutes perpetual movement, and is clearly inspired by the ideas of Nietzsche, although it is significant that what the restless gipsy creates at the end of the poem is not the Superman, although that figure is intro-duced indirectly and dismissed, but art in the form of music. Following Nietzsche the gipsy, who is not himself a Greek by race, progressively rejects the social conventions, religion and established tradition on which Greek society at the turn of the century was based. Witnessing the papyrus relics of ancient Greek culture being loaded on to ships to be taken to the west, shortly before Constantinople is due to fall to the

Turks, he hears the appeal of the 'beautiful ancients' and the claim of this most intractable bedrock of the modern Greek tradition to continued life and veneration. In words that must have taken some courage to write, in the first decade of the 20th century, Palamás' gipsy bids a tender farewell to ancient Greece:

> What if you are indeed immortal?
> The life that is all alive
> once only
> did you live as created beings
> with bodies whole
> in your blessèd country's
> air and sun;
> a different air and different sun
> are now for you; and nevermore
> will you live again your lives,
> you ghosts!

(Canto 5)

Although its strategy is mostly negative, this poem of Palamás goes to the heart of the modern Greek's attempt to define his identity by means of tradition. Later poets have attempted similar projects in very different ways. Ritsos, in the long poem *Romiosíni* already mentioned, defines the 'Greekness' of the work's title in terms of popular traditions and a primitive unity between the Greek peasant or worker and the landscape out of which he has eked a living for centuries; Elytis in *To 'Axion Estí* (1959) adds to these elements of tradition a sustained invocation to the Orthodox liturgy and Christian Byzantine literature, but in their formal aspects only. Whether seen in its 'high' culture perspective as 'Hellenism' or in its 'low' culture perspective as 'Romiosini' (from the popular word used by Greeks, before independence, to designate themselves, *Romií*), the attempt to define Greek culture is a frequent theme both of poetry and prose. Since the appeal to tradition as a means of validating a national identity is a matter of *creating* rather than truly of *discovering* such an identity, each exploration of the theme results in a significantly different version of what has been sought. Since the quest for identity through the traditions of the past is in fact the progressive accumulation of a *modern* Greek tradition, its goal remains necessarily elusive.

21

The stage of the quest reached today was put epigramatically by the novelist Vasílis Vasilikós, in a BBC television programme broadcast in 1984. Asked to define *Romiosíni*, Vasilikós replied, 'The Greeks have a word for it. But they don't have . . . it.'

This brief survey has necessarily been schematic, and much has had to be left out. But I have tried to sketch, however cursorily, what seem to me to be the main lines of development and the most important contrasts and continuities in Greek literature since national independence. The result is still overburdened, I realise, with names and dates, but in the absence of a convenient reference book — even in Greek — there seems no way of avoiding this. I hope in any case to have given some idea of the variety of Modern Greek literature, as well as of its connections with and differences from the more familiar literatures of the West.

NOTES

1. On this period specifically see Henderson, G. P., *The Revival of Greek Thought, 1620-1820*. Albany, N.Y.: State University of New York Press, 1970.
   The only satisfactory general reference book on modern Greek literature in English is Politis, Linos. *A History of Modern Greek Literature*. [Translated by Robert Liddell.] Oxford: Clarendon Press, 1973.
2. Translated as Emmanuel Royidis, *Pope Joan* by Lawrence Durrell. New York: Dutton, 1960; London: Overlook Press, 1984.
3. Papadiamandis, Alexandros. *The Murderess*. Translated by Peter Levi. London and New York: Writers and Readers, 1983. Unfortunately part of the text has been displaced on pp. 121-4, so that the end of the novel has become garbled.
4. Karkavitsas, Andreas, *The Beggar*, translated, with notes, by William F. Wyatt, Jr., with an appendix by P. D. Mastrodimítris. New York: Caratzas, 1982.
5. Georgios M. Vizyenos, My Mother's Sin and Other Stories, translated, with notes, William F. Wyatt, Jr., with an introduction by Roderick Beaton. University Press of New England, 1988.
6. The best translations are Palamas, Kostis. *The Twelve Lays of the Gipsy*, translated with an introduction by George Thomson. London: Lawrence and Wishart, 1969; and *The King's Flute*, translated by Theodore Ph. Stephanides and George C. Katsimbalis (Preface by Charles Diehl, introduction by E. P. Papanútsos). Athens: Ídrima Kostí Palamá, 1982. For a readable and informed study of the poet in English see Fletcher, Robin. *Kostes Palamas: a Great Modern Greek Poet — His Life, His Work and His Struggle for Demoticism*. Athens: Ídrima Kostí Palamá, 1984.
7. All Kazantzákis' novels are available in English translation, published by Faber and Faber (London). His other major work available in English is *The Odyssey: a Modern Sequel*, translated, with introduction, synopsis

and notes, by Kimon Friar. New York: Simon and Schuster; London: Secker and Warburg, 1958.

The best studies of Kazantzákis in English are Bien, Peter. *Kazantzakis and the Linguistic Revolution in Greek Literature.* Princeton, N.J.: Princeton University Press, [1972]; and Bien, Peter. *Nikos Kazantzakis. Columbia Essays on Modern Writers, no. 62.* New York: Columbia University Press, 1972.

8. See Sikelianos, Angelos. *Selected Poems,* translated and introduced by Edmund Keeley and Philip Sherrard. Princeton, N.J.: Princeton University Press, 1979; London: Allen and Unwin, 1980.

9. Cavafy, C. P. [Kaváfis, K. P.] *Collected Poems,* translated by Edmund Keeley and Philip Sherrard; edited by George Savidis. Princeton, N.J.: Princeton University Press; London: The Hogarth Press, 1975. This is the fullest available edition of Cavafy in English, and the only one to benefit from George Savidis' notes on metre, historical allusions, drafts, revisions and first publication for each poem. The London edition has the English text only.

The best study of Cavafy in English remains Keeley, Edmund. *Cavafy's Alexandria: Study of a Myth in Progress.* Cambridge, Mass.: Harvard University Press, 1976; London: Hogarth Press, 1977.

10. Translated by Peter Bien. Hanover, New Hampshire: University Press of New England, 1977, London: Quartet, 1987.

11. Translated as *Aeolia* by I. D. Scott-Kilvert, with a preface by Lawrence Durrell. New York: Vanguard Press, 1957. (Also published in England with the title *Beyond the Aegean.*)

12. Included in Seferis, George [Yiórgos]. *Collected Poems.* Translated and edited, with an introduction, by Edmund Keeley and Philip Sherrard. [Expanded edition.] London: Anvil Press Poetry, 1982.

13. See Elytis, Odysseus [Elítis, Odisséas]. *The Axion Esti,* translated and annotated by Edmund Keeley and George Savidis. Pittsburgh: University of Pittsburgh Press, 1974; London: Anvil Press, 1980; Elytis, Odysseus, *Selected Poems,* chosen and introduced by Edmund Keeley and Philip Sherrard; translated by Edmund Keeley et al. New York: Viking Press; London: Anvil Press Poetry, 1982; and Elytis, Odysseus, *The Sovereign Sun: Selected Poems,* translated with an introduction and notes by Kimon Friar. Philadelphia: Temple University Press, 1974.

14. Rítsos' collected works in Greek now run to seven large volumes. Selections from these can be found in the following translations: Ritsos, Yiannis. *Ritsos in Parentheses,* translated with an introduction by Edmund Keeley. Princeton, N.J.: Princeton University Press, 1979; Ritsos, Yiannis. *Scripture of the Blind.* Translated with an introduction by Kimon Friar and Kostas Myrsiades. Columbus, Ohio: Ohio State University Press, 1979; and Ritsos, Yiannis. *Selected Poems.* Translated by Nikos Stangos with an introduction by Peter Bien. Harmondsworth, Middlesex, England and Baltimore: Penguin Books, 1974 (reprinted by Efstathiadis, Athens).

15. See Sahtouris, Miltos. *Selected Poems,* translated with an introduction by Kimon Friar. Old Chatham, N.Y.: Sachem Press, 1982; Sinopoulos, Takis. *Landscape of Death: The Selected Poems of Tákis Sinópoulos,* translated, with an introduction, by Kimon Friar. Columbus, Ohio: Ohio State University Press, 1979; and Sinopoulos, Takis. *Selected Poems,* translated, with an introduction, by John Stathatos. London: Oxus Press, 1981.

16. Translated by Kay Cicellis. New York: Alfred A. Knopf, 1974.

17. Taktsis, Kostas, *The Third Wedding,* translated by Leslie Finer. London: Alan Ross, 1967; Harmondsworth, Middlesex, England: Penguin Books, 1969 [out of print]. Re-translated as *The Third Wedding Wreath,* with an

23

introduction, by John Chioles. Athens: Hermes [= Ermís], 1985.

18. See Savidis, George P., 'The Burden of the Past and the Greek Poet'. Grand Street 4 (1985): 164–90; 5 (1986): 153–74.
19. Kornaros, Vitzentzos, *Erotokritos*, translated by Theodore Ph. Stephanides, Athens, Papaziosis Publishers, 1984 (distributed by Merlin Press).
20. There is still no English translation of even selections from the poetry of Solomós, although the following critical studies include useful translated extracts: Jenkins, Romilly. *Dionysius Solomos*. Cambridge, England: Cambridge University Press, 1940; Athens: Denise Harvey, 1981; Raizis, M. Byron. *Dionysios Solomos*. Twayne's World Authors Series, no. 193. New York: Twayne, 1972; and Beaton, Roderick. 'Dionysios Solomos: the Tree of Poetry'. Byzantine and Modern Greek Studies 2 (1976): 161–82.
21. Myrivilis, Stratis. *Vasilis Arvanitis*, translated by Pavlos Andronikos. Armidale, N.S.W. [Australia]: The University of New England Publishing Unit, 1983.
22 See Beaton, Roderick. *Folk Poetry of Modern Greece*. Cambridge: Cambridge University Press, 1980, especially pp. 58–64.

KATHAREVOUSA (c. 1800–1974)
AN OBITUARY FOR AN OFFICIAL LANGUAGE

Peter Mackridge

The son of a great poet used to say that the profitless burden which he was condemned by irrevocable ill fortune to bear on his shoulders throughout his life was his father's name. The great and useless load which we Greeks are condemned by irrevocable ill fortune to bear on our puny shoulders is the great and glorious, but heavy and burdensome name of our great forefathers, with all the obligations that it entails.

Vernardakis (1884: 441)

The Greek language question, which has come near to a solution only during the last fifteen years after dogging Greek culture for a century and a half, has been an inevitable concomitant of the problems faced by the Greeks in establishing a relationship with their ancient predecessors. The aim of this chapter is to provide a chronicle of events in the history of the language controversy, especially during this century, summarizing and commenting on its causes and on the arguments put forward, and attempting to assess the successes and failures of each side in the dispute.

First we must attempt some definitions. Until 1974 there was a situation of diglossia in Greece: that is, two varieties of the same language were used for different purposes (this is not to be confused with bilingualism, in which two different languages are used in the same country); 'the two forms interpenetrate continuously and yet are thought of as mutually exclusive' (Alexiou 1982: 178). These two varieties are normally known as demotic and *katharevousa*. Demotic (literally 'the people's language') is the ordinary spoken language that developed naturally from the *koine* ('common language') of Hellenistic and Roman times (roughly, the

25

period between the fourth century B.C. and the fourth century A.D.); nevertheless, the term 'demotic' is often used to refer especially to that particular version of the language which developed as the everyday spoken language of the large urban centres and was cultivated by literary writers during the nineteenth and twentieth centuries. Ever since Hellenistic times, however, most writers had avoided using the spoken language in their works, and there developed a tradition of writing in a language that represented a compromise between the spoken language of the time and the Greek of the Classical period (fifth and fourth centuries B.C.). On the eve of Greece's independence in the early nineteenth century a written language was codified that continued this tradition of diglossia, in that it was again a mixture of ancient and modern features: it was this written language that came to be known as *katharevousa* (literally 'purifying language', since it represented an attempt to purge the modern language of words which it had taken from foreign languages and to reinstate much of the lexical and grammatical wealth of the ancient language which had been lost or altered during the previous two millennia).

Few Greek intellectuals have wanted to believe or admit that Ancient and Modern Greek are not one and the same language. Indeed, many have objected to the very term 'Modern Greek', which implies that Greek can be divided up on a chronological basis. One of the tenets of official Greek ideology, subscribed to by the intellectual establishment since the founding of the Greek state in 1821, is the unbroken continuity of Greek culture since Classical times. Whatever the validity of this tenet, it has often led to a perverse refusal to acknowledge the influence of the passage of time on language and culture; indeed, any acknowledgement of such an influence has sometimes been considered tantamount to casting doubt on the connection between the Ancient and the Modern Greeks. Greek intellectuals have usually been torn between pride in their descent from the ancients and regret that they have been born too late to participate in the matchless civilization that their forefathers created.

The close connections between Classical Greek (and even more the *koine* used in the New Testament) and modern demotic are as remarkable as they are clear to see. Modern

Italian is considered to be very close to Latin (far closer than is French, for instance), but — to confine ourselves to noun declension — it has not only lost one of the ancient genders (neuter), but its nouns are no longer inflected for case, the whole Latin system of nominative, vocative, accusative, genitive, dative, and ablative having disappeared without trace. Demotic Greek, on the other hand, not only preserves all three ancient genders, but has also kept the ancient case system almost intact, having lost only one of the cases of Ancient Greek (the dative). These examples can be taken as typical of the conservative nature of Modern Greek, in which many more features of vocabulary and grammar have remained practically unchanged over two thousand years than is the case in most other European languages.[1] As far as the vocabulary and morphology are concerned, then, the gap between Ancient and Modern Greek is so small that there has always been a temptation to bridge it by the revival or retrieval of those ancient features that have been lost or changed — the rehellenization of a language that has become tainted by non-Hellenic features. The Greek intellectuals of the nineteenth century who were chiefly responsible for the development of *katharevousa* were greatly assisted by a general tendency among the Greeks to overlook changes in syntax, and especially changes in pronunciation, since ancient times. Greeks have traditionally pronounced Ancient Greek in the same way as they pronounce their own language, and few Greek linguists have had the courage to acknowledge the systematic sound-changes which took place in Greek during the centuries after the Classical period and which had a crucial influence on the vocabulary and grammar of the language, bringing about many of the changes that the purists were trying to reverse. Mirambel (1964: 416–7) has pointed out the contradiction that *katharevousa* took over much of the vocabulary and grammar of Ancient Greek without the pronunciation that should properly have gone with them; nevertheless, he adds rather wickedly, the fact that the Modern Greeks are alone in pronouncing Ancient Greek in the way they do has led them to believe that they are the only true heirs of ancient Hellenism.

One should not, however, underestimate the linguistic dilemma faced by Greek intellectuals around the time of

the Greek independence movement. One of their prime tasks
was to facilitate the transition from an essentially oral to an
essentially literate culture as the government of the country
passed from foreign hands (which wrote in a foreign language)
to those of Greeks who would have to use some form of
Greek as the language of law, administration, and education.
It seemed absurd to the new Greek establishment that the
language of the illiterate folk should – or even could – be
employed without alteration in the official documents of the
new state, especially since most writing had traditionally
been done in a form of Greek partly modelled on the ancient
language. Moreover, as a matter of national prestige – to
impress the Europeans with their respect for their ancient
heritage – it seemed imperative that the Greeks should not
ignore the ancient tongue when devising their official modern
language.

Katharevousa, then, and specifically the version of the
written language that had been refined by Adamandios
Korais (1748–1833), became *de facto* the language of the
Greek state from its very first pronouncements during the
War of Independence against the Ottoman Empire (1821–
1828). With the exception of sporadic expressions of dissent,
chiefly from inhabitants of the Ionian Islands, which were
not incorporated into the Greek state until 1863, the
exclusion of demotic from the official life of Greece remained
unchallenged for sixty years after the War of Independence.
This does not however mean that there was no language
controversy, but that the disputes were generally confined to
those among proponents of various compromises between
the ancient and the modern languages. The two chief disputes
took place during the 1850s and the 1880s, each of them
provoked (apart from pronounced personal animosities) by
dissatisfaction at the lamentable way in which the language
was being written, each writer displaying scant regard for the
rules of either Ancient or Modern Greek in their arbitrary
mixture of the two languages. In each case the dispute began
with a writer (Panayotis Soutsos [1853] and Konstandinos
Kondos [1882]) publishing a book in which he pointed out
'solecisms' in other mens' writings and called for the written
language to be made to conform closer to ancient rules. It is
interesting to notice how, as the generations went by between
the 1820s, the 1850s, and the 1880s, there was increasing

dissatisfaction with the version of Greek proposed by Korais: the instigators of each of these two disputes looked upon the increased archaization of the modern written language as being 'progressive', seeing Korais as too 'conservative' for contemporary tastes because, working during the period of Greek servitude, he was unwilling to depart sufficiently far from the spoken language. For these men, no less than Korais, believed in 'progress' towards an ideal of ancient Greek perfection. It is significant, however, that both Soutsos and Kondos stated that it would be preferable to use demotic than bad *katharevousa* (Soutsos 1853: 39ff.; Kondos 1882: 184); in this they were unwittingly admitting to the impossibility of their venture, for what was the criterion of good *katharevousa* when the language consisted of an arbitrary mixture of elements from two different grammars? Each of these pedants provoked a series of attacks and counter-attacks containing nit-picking, casuistic criticisms of alleged mistakes in their opponents' writings, sometimes with humour but always with spiteful jealousy which on occasion led to libel-suits. In sum, all these writers practised precisely the linguistic anarchy that they professed to attack, and all their arguments led to the same impasse.

During and between these two disputes few voices were raised on more essential matters. One such was that of a rare demoticist, Konemenos, who wrote, in demotic, that 'language is a means, not an end' (1873: 6), and that the Greek's adherence to ancient models, in language as in everything else, was 'keeping us static and unhealthy'. 'We need,' he continued, 'to come out from inside the tombs, to come out from under the yoke, to breathe, to live, to search for a new world, and to form our own new culture' (ibid., 55). These words look forward to a crucial development that took place fifteen years later, when Psycharis published *My Journey* (1888), the manifesto that inaugurated the demoticist movement. This polemical book, a cross between a sociolinguistic study and a travelogue of a journey around the Greek-speaking world, was written in a homogeneous demotic devised by the author himself, who intended it as a model for all future writing. Psycharis set the language question on a new footing by writing the following: 'The language question is a political question: what the army is fighting to achieve for our physical frontiers, the language wants to achieve for our intellectual frontiers: both must go far and increase their scope. Together we shall prosper some day' (1971: 201). In this way Psycharis, referring to the Greeks' struggles to liberate their brethren who were still living under the Ottoman yoke, linked the language question to the survival and prosperity of the Greeks as a nation, and this link has remained intact ever since.

Meanwhile demotic, which (apart from a sterile half-century between 1830 and 1880 in Athens, when poets were vainly attempting to write in *katharevousa*) had been the normal language of poetry for centuries, was being intensively cultivated by a new generation of poets in Athens, and Psycharis' book soon persuaded prosewriters to compose their stories and novels in demotic too. There was an intense nationalistic literary activity in demotic, which went hand in hand with the intellectuals' discovery of and admiration for folk life and traditions, and the patriotic nature of this literature made it increasingly absurd that Greek national literature (including even the National Anthem) was written in anything other than what was supposed to be the national language. Nevertheless, while there was an inevitable barrage of criticisms and denunciations of Psycharis' book, the language question really became an important national issue in the first decade of the twentieth century, when for the first time the establishment felt seriously threatened by the movement to establish demotic officially as the national language.

A succession of events provided a springboard for an intense and often violent controversy, in which for the first time the proponents of *katharevousa* were really forced to defend their entrenched position. In 1901 A. Pallis translated the Gospels into demotic (this was the second time this had been done: the first published demotic translation of the New Testament, in 1638, was suppressed and never reprinted). The serialization of his translation in an Athens newspaper provoked protests from university students, who alleged that Hellenism, the 'sublime language' of the Greeks, and the Holy Gospels themselves were being brought into ridicule. The protestors clashed with police, who were defending the freedom of speech, and eight demonstrators were killed. The Gospel Riots provided the excuse for the purists to mount a campaign of vilification against the demoticists (often known at this time as *malliari*, or 'hairies', because of the rather Bohemian appearance of some of them): Pallis' translation of the Gospels (like that of 1638) were felt to be an assault on the Orthodox Church, especially since vernacular Bible translations were associated with Protestantism, a link made all the more plausible by the fact that Pallis lived in England. More grist was provided for the purists' mill by events in 1903, when the Greek National Theatre put on a production of Aeschylus' *Oresteia* in demotic translation at the Herod Atticus Theatre in Athens. More demonstrations resulted, and the production had to be discontinued. The demoticists could now be accused not only of atheism, but of attempting to drive a wedge between Ancient and Modern Greek culture – a paradoxical allegation, since demotic translations clearly brought the ancient dramas close to the contemporary audience; but the fact that the Bible and Classical texts were being translated implied the uncomfortable truth that the purists wanted to ignore: that most Greeks could not understand these texts in the original.

At the same time a tug-of-war was taking place in Macedonia between the Greeks and the Bulgarians as to who would take control of the region when the Ottoman occupiers departed. Part of the campaign of denigration against the demoticists, quite apart from a whole mythology of alleged hyper-demotic forms that no demoticist had ever written, was now that they were in the pay of the Russians, and that *malliarismos* ('hairy-ism') was part of a pan-Slavist plot to break up the unified Greek language into dialects, thus weakening the bonds between Greeks and making them easy prey to Russian and Bulgarian expansionism. (Allegations that the demoticists were in receipt of Russian roubles gained greater potency with the Bolshevik Revolution of 1917, and again with the Soviet takeover of three out of four of Greece's neighbours – Albania, Bulgaria, and Yugoslavia – at the end of the Second World War). Nevertheless, the demoticists could argue, with considerable evidence to support them, that it was precisely the teaching of Ancient Greek and *katharevousa* rather than demotic in the Greek schools in Macedonia that was driving children there to attend the Bulgarian schools, where they were indeed taught a unified language. It was in this context that the first demoticist society was founded, in 1905, with the name 'The

National Language Society'. Among the demands made in this short-lived society's manifesto was that demotic should be immediately introduced into primary schools, both in the Kingdom of Greece and in Macedonia, and that ultimately 'our living national language should become the written language of the Greek race' (*Etairia* 1905: 15).[2]

In 1907 the socialist Skliros published a book entitled *Our Social Problem*, in which, among other things, he argued that the national language could not be reformed without thorough changes in society, and criticized the bourgeois demoticists for trying to convert the ruling class rather than addressing the people. In the ensuing discussion in the columns of the demoticist magazine *Noumas* (founded in 1903), the correspondents – all of them demoticists – were clearly divided into nationalists, who saw the language question as a cultural and educational matter vital to the survival and prosperity of the whole nation, particularly in its struggle against the Turks, and socialists, who saw it as a social and political matter that concerned the class struggle and the domination of the ruling clique. In 1910 the Educational Society was founded, a 'demoticist lobby' (Bien 1972: 93) which lasted until 1929 and was to have an enduring influence on the language question and indeed on the development of the Greek language itself, even though its chief specific goal was the reform of primary education. For most of its existence it managed to distance itself both from the intransigent followers of Psycharis and from the socialist demoticists; its pronouncements were sober and carefully thought out, and its language was a demotic that made some practical concessions to *katharevousa* which coincided with normal educated spoken usage.

Reaction against the progress of demoticism reached a peak in 1911. Three years previously a young demoticist educationalist, A. Delmouzos, had set up in the town of Volos the first public high school for girls in Greece. But his progressive educational ideas and his use of demotic as the sole medium of teaching so incensed the local bishop that he stirred up the local populace to demand the closure of the school. This strategy was successful, a new weapon having been added to the establishment's armory against demoticism, besides atheism and anti-national behaviour: the physical and moral corruption of children. (At the subsequent trial, at which the bishop equated 'hairy-ism, anarchism, socialism, atheism, and freemasonry' (Dimaras 1974: 106), Delmouzos was acquitted of all charges for lack of evidence.) Later in the same year, after a long and heated debate in Parliament, the reactionaries won a resounding victory: the Greek Constitution of 1911 (in most respects a fairly liberal one) contained, for the first time, a clause specifying an 'official language'. Article 107 stated: 'The official language of the state is that in which the constitution and the laws of Greece are drawn up; any intervention to corrupt it is forbidden.' The highly ambiguous phraseology of this clause subtly avoids the difficulty of defining *katharevousa* by simply not mentioning it. In 1915 Venizelos, who had been Prime Minister at the time when the Constitution was drawn up, claimed in a newspaper interview that, although he had been forced to give way to the reactionaries in 1911, he had deliberately engineered the ambiguity of the clause: 'The formulation of the provision on the language is sophistic. As soon as laws are enacted in demotic, demotic will be the official language' (Moschonas 1975: xxix). Venizelos' assertion must be considered as sophistic as the clause itself, especially in view of the fact that the first piece of legislation drafted in demotic was not passed until 1977. Be that as it may, Article 107 of 1911 was a powerful blow against demoticism, and, although it was omitted from the 1927 constitution, it reappeared in the constitutions of 1952 and 1968 (in the latter, 'the Colonels' Constitution', the first phrase was amplified to read, 'The official language of the state and of education').

Nevertheless, when Venizelos began his second premiership in 1917 as leader of a pro-Entente and anti-monarchist government, he appointed the three leading members of the demoticist Educational Society to key educational posts: Dimitris Glinos became General Secretary of the Ministry of Education, and Manolis Triandaphyllidis and Alexandros Delmouzos took up posts specially created for them as Chief Supervisors of Primary Education. Under their guidance, demotic was introduced as the sole language of instruction and of study in the first four grades of primary school, and special school readers and other textbooks were written for the purpose. The Macedonian problem was no doubt one of the chief reasons for these reforms: the non-Greek-speaking population of the province (which had been gained by Greece in the Balkan Wars against Turkey and Bulgaria in 1912–13) were still proving resistant to the Greek educational system (cf. Triandaphyllidis 1982: 133–5; Moschonas 1975: xxx). Since the Educational Society had thrown in its lot with a single political party, however, it was inevitable that its reforms would be undone as soon as that party fell from power, which is what happened in 1920, when the electorate voted overwhelmingly against Venizelos' expansionist enterprise in Asia Minor. Ever after, until 1974, there was to be a successive alternation of moves to reduce or increase the presence of demotic in primary schools, although demotic never completely lost the foothold it had gained in 1917. The Educational Society itself never won any further victories, and, having become identified with a certain kind of establishment, it attracted constant criticism not only from the *katharevousa* supporters but from rival demoticists such as the followers of Psycharis, each group of demoticists accusing the other both of laying down the law and of diverging from its own linguistic orthodoxy (Moschonas 1975: xlviii–xlix).

Two months before the establishment of Greece's first Fascist dictatorship, in April 1925, a 'National Conference' was convened by various conservative religious and cultural organizations 'to combat the enemies and corrupters of Religion, Language, Family, Property, Morals, National Consciousness, and the Fatherland' (Dimaras 1974: 143–4): the demoticists, it seems, were being used as scapegoats for the national disaster of 1922, when Greece was crushingly defeated by the Turks, with the result that the continuous presence of Greeks in Asia Minor since pre-Classical times was brought to an abrupt and violent end as one and a half million Greeks were deported to Greece. The dictator Pangalos himself announced in 1925 that 'a large proportion of the hairies are Communists, and they will be prosecuted' (Moschonas 1975: lix); in 1926 a Royalist newspaper linked 'hairy-ism' and Communism as undermining the foundations of the state (Moschonas 1975: lxvi), while the leading academic supporter of *katharevousa*, Professor G. N. Hadzidakis, linked it with 'cosmopolitanism' and feminism (Triandaphyllidis 1982: liii–liv). Educationalist demoticists

34

such as Triandaphyllidis and Delmouzos were therefore obliged to spend much of their time writing articles arguing that there was no connection between demoticism and Communism.

Ironically enough, the Greek Communist Party was still normally employing *katharevousa* during this period. Although the inaugural programme of the Socialist Labour Party of Greece (founded in 1918 and changing its name to Communist Party of Greece in 1924) contained a demand for the abolition of the language provision in the Constitution and the introduction of demotic throughout education (Moschonas 1975: lxxiii), the subsequent official texts of the Party make little or no mention of the language question between 1918 and 1928 (ibid., lxxiv) – no doubt because such a problem was unfamiliar to its Soviet steersmen. The official Party newspaper, *Rizospastis*, was produced in *katharevousa* until 1927, the same year in which the Party issued its last official document in that language (ibid., lxxiv–lxxviii). This is a powerful indication that – at least until 1927 – it was not obvious that one had to be a demoticist in order to be progressive. It was felt that the masses could best be appealed to in a language that had a reputation for seriousness; indeed, for many left-wingers, demoticism was tainted as being a bourgeois movement. Nevertheless, the gradual *rapprochement* between the Communist Party and the demoticist movement around 1927 may well be connected with the sudden conversion to Marxism in 1926 of one of the leading lights of the Educational Society, Dimitris Glinos.

The same years saw a shift in the situation of many important demoticists. Immediately after the fall of Pangalos in 1926, Manolis Triandaphyllidis was appointed Professor of Linguistics at the newly-founded University of Salonica, whose Arts Faculty immediately established demotic as the medium of teaching. Alexandros Delmouzos took up a post as Professor of Education at the same university in 1929: thus the liberals of the Educational Society, from their position of power, believed that they had won their battle and fell quiet. The Society ceased to function altogether in 1929, two years after it was taken over by Marxists led by Glinos. Also in 1929 Psycharis died, and *Noumas*, the magazine that had so strongly supported his linguistic ideas for two and a half decades, ceased publication in 1931.

Nevertheless, apart from Salonica University, demotic had only been introduced into the first grades of primary school, and, although the Constitution of 1927 made no mention of an official language, *katharevousa* remained the sole language of administration. Meanwhile the first half of the 1930s saw an increase in the attempts of compromisers to have the spoken language of educated Athenians (rather than the supposedly pan-Hellenic and slightly more rural variety of the Educational Society) imposed as official language.

The Metaxas dictatorship, which lasted from 1936 until it collapsed with the German invasion of April 1941, was unexpectedly favourable towards demoticism despite its ruthless anti-Communism and anti-Liberalism. This was because of Metaxas' own personal commitment to educational reform as part of his attempt to instil discipline into Greek society, and his support of the 'language of the people' was consistent with his general populism. As early as the second month of his dictatorship (September 1936), he told a newspaper in an interview that it was wrong to identify demoticism with Communism: rather, it was 'a purely national movement' (Moschonas 1975: xcvii). He appointed himself Minister of Education in November 1938, and in the following month sent an encyclical to teachers in which he made it clear that he would not tolerate any failure to teach 'the mother tongue' in the first four grades of primary school (Christidis 1974: clxvi–clxvii). In the same month his ministry set up a committee, chaired by Triandaphyllidis, to compile a Modern Greek Grammar (Triandaphyllidis 1982: lxiv). In a draft prologue to the grammar, not eventually included in the published version, Metaxas himself wrote that 'grammatical rules will curtail the [Greeks'] overdeveloped individuality' and provide the people with 'linguistic discipline' (Moschonas 1975: xcviii). Unfortunately for the demoticist movement, which now saw the finest linguist among its adherents appointed to draw up a 'state grammar', this monumental *Modern Greek Grammar* was not published until June 1941: the vast majority of the Greek population were obviously too preoccupied by the German invasion of two months previously to give much thought to grammar.

There was a small group of men, however, for whom, amid the famine and brutality of the Axis Occupation, the language question was of vital importance. These men were the

36

professors of the Faculty of Arts at the University of Athens, who had found themselves frustratingly powerless onlookers at Metaxas' professed love for demotic. Metaxas having died on the eve of the German invasion, they found the opportunity to reassert the traditional established values of purism. In November 1941 Professor I. Kakridis was censured by the Dean of the Faculty for republishing a talk in demotic and in a slightly simplified orthography (the 'monotonic', or 'single-accent' system). For this, and for some of the ideas on Classical education contained in the talk, Kakridis was punished with two months' suspension from duties in July 1942 (Dimaras 1974: 193–202). During the 'Trial of the Accents' one of Kakridis' accusers even went so far as to link demoticism with dictatorship, asserting that the demoticists 'have always attempted to impose their ideas by *coup d'état* and during periods when either dictatorial régimes were functioning in our country or irregularities prevailed' (Moschonas 1975: xcix).

Meanwhile, in the mountains, each of the chief Resistance groups proclaimed itself in favour of demotic: the Liberal EDES announced in 1943 that demotic would be the sole language of education, while the Communist-led EAM could maintain in 1944 that in the areas under its control demotic was already the language of education, legislation, the law courts, and of official documents, although in practice there were many exceptions (ibid., c–ci). During the Civil War (even from December 1944 onwards) there was a reversion to the polarization of twenty years before (ibid., civ).

Soon after the Liberal George Papandreou became Prime Minister in 1963, he appointed himself Minister of Education, and under his leadership there was established a policy of 'equal rights' for *katharevousa* and demotic throughout education, though *katharevousa* remained constitutionally the official language. The military dictatorship of 1967–74 reversed this policy, and shored up the *katharevousa* edifice by adulterating the language of those primary school text-books which were supposed to be written in demotic. A widely circulated pamphlet published in 1973 by the General Staff of the Armed Forces, entitled *National Language*, repeated all the old arguments against demotic, stressing its alleged link with Communism and asserting that it was not really a language at all.

The Conservative government of Karamanlis, which succeeded the dictatorship in 1974, began to use demotic for various purposes from the outset. Its Constitution of 1975 wisely omitted to mention an official language, and various laws of 1976 laid down demotic as the sole language of education and of the whole administration. Nevertheless most legal texts have continued to be formulated in *katharevousa*, and as recently as March 1986 the Greek Parliament, while ratifying for the first time a demotic translation of the Constitution, ruled that the original text retains legal precedence for the purposes of interpretation.

Having been reduced for most of the last few decades to being a purely administrative language (*Kanzleisprache*), *katharevousa* has now all but vanished; the dead skin that Modern Greek had artificially been prevented from sloughing off has fallen away, allowing the language a greater freedom of movement and development. It was poets and then prose-writers who first turned their backs on it in the nineteenth century, and it was at least partly on the demotic that had been cultivated in literature by the writers of the nineteenth and early twentieth centuries that the Educational Society based its version of the language from 1910 onwards; this version, in turn, became enshrined in what many people have referred to as the 'state grammar' of 1941; and it was a simplified précis of this grammar that was issued by the government to schoolteachers and civil servants in 1976 to help them to teach and to formulate documents in demotic. Thus have the policies of the Educational Society, three score years and ten after its foundation, come to fruition, and their version of demotic has not only been accepted *de facto* by the state as the official language of Greece, but it had already deeply influenced the practice of writers in demotic for many decades.

After this chronicle of events, one clearly needs to ask both why there should ever have been a language question in the first place, and what were the arguments put forward by the proponents of the different versions of the language.

Arnold Toynbee wrote that 'the *katharevousa* is a product of the Modern Greeks' mistrust of themselves in the face of Hellenic predecessors for whom they have felt themselves to be no match' (1981: 266). There is no doubt that Greek diglossia, or 'schizoglossia' (Petrounias 1978: 197), is the result, through the ages, of later Greeks' feelings of inferiority in relation to their ancestors. *Katharevousa* was like a pidgin that the Modern Greek intellectuals developed in order to be able to converse with the Ancient Greeks, who, they seem to have believed, were the true natives of Greece; this conversation was inevitably doomed to remain one-sided. Moreover, not only did the majority of Modern Greeks fail to learn Ancient Greek satisfactorily, but they also seemed resistant to learning *katharevousa*, a situation that contrasts with the enthusiasm of the Israelis to learn modern Hebrew, the official language of the state devised by Jewish intellectuals not long before the state was founded.

The basis of the *katharevousa* movement in the nineteenth century was a feeling among Greek intellectuals, educated in western Europe, that the Ancient Greek language was an instrument of such supreme perfection that any deviation from it was a cause for regret and shame. Whether they strongly argued in favour of a complete return to Ancient Greek or for some compromise between the ancient and modern languages, many of them believed that through an imitation of the language of the ancients, the universally admired culture of Classical Hellas would spontaneously flower again. The plight of a desperately poor, underdeveloped country emerging out of centuries of oppression awakened both a Romantic nostalgia for a myth of bygone glory and a blinkered optimism about the possibilities of future progress. The worst consequence of the obvious gap between ancient glory and modern squalor was perhaps a metaphysical obsession with decay and a desire for purity and permanence, which led many intellectuals to believe that history could be ignored. As Triandaphyllidis pointed out, the adherents of *katharevousa* refused to see Ancient Greek culture as the product of a specific time and circumstances (1982: 95). Mirambel has stressed the inextricable link in the purists' minds between 'the prestige of the ancient' and 'the primacy of the written', since Ancient Greek is only known through the written word (1964: 408); there has been a widespread sense in Greece that *scripta manent*, while oral language consists of evanescent 'winged words'.

Richard Rorty has talked of 'intellectual history viewed as the history of metaphor' (1986: 6). One of the failings of the histories of the Greek language from ancient to modern times has been their concentration on changes in or the preservation of formal structures — phonetics and morphology — to the exclusion of semantic changes: metaphor as a process of semantic change is overlooked. This is exemplified in the standard *Etymological Dictionary of Common Modern Greek* (1967) by Andriotis, a demoticist, who in his entries on words of Ancient Greek origin confines his discussion purely to changes in form, not sense. Such a widespread concentration on form at the expense of content in Greece has made it possible for the purists to believe that they would think (and therefore be) like the Ancient Greeks by imitating the formal structures of the latter's language. This has led to the development of *katharevousa* as a dressing-up of western European concepts in ethnic garb, and the disguising of a new language behind an ancient mask; often Ancient Greek words have been revived in modern times with a new meaning (for examples see Mackridge 1985: 312–13). Thus the linguistic racism of *katharevousa* is all surface: as long as a word *looks* as if it could be Ancient Greek, one does not question its right of domicile, but if there is a possibility that it could be of non-Greek origin, then it must be expelled as an illegal immigrant. As for concepts and meanings, despite the early demoticists' dissatisfaction that *katharevousa* was literally translated from French (the fact that it was modelled on French was admitted by some purists, e.g. Hadzidakis [1907b: 32]), a later demoticist such as Andriotis could admit in 1932 that, 'even more than Ancient Greek, the French language has been the *alma mater* of the cultural life of Modern Greece' (1976: 317).

Katharevousa has often been disparagingly described as a 'bourgeois language'. Moschonas, however, is right to point out that demoticists and purists alike have been generally of bourgeois backgrounds and have subscribed to a bourgeois ideology, the demoticists simply trying to find a way of making the existing system work more efficiently (1985: xiv); it should be noted, for instance, that ten out of the eleven participants in the *Noumas* discussion on demoticism and socialism in 1907–9 — both nationalists and socialists — were resident outside Greece (Stavridi-Patrikiou 1976: xxx), and most of the chief demoticists of the generation of 1880 were permanent expatriates, including Psycharis, who like Korais before him resided permanently in Paris. These men were hardly from anything but bourgeois or aristocratic back-grounds. Tziovas describes the language controversy in terms of a conflict over the appropriation of authority to form a Greek national identity (1985: 272), and personal ambition played a large part in the conflict.

Mirambel wrote that the Greeks 'have made language serve less the expression of intellectual needs and mutual compre-hension than the desire to distinguish themselves from each other' (1937: 44). *Katharevousa* has certainly been a tool used by a rising class to secure its gains. Those people from peasant families who had managed to complete their education and go to university tended to be content with *katharevousa*, which was the emblem of their social advancement and set them apart from the ignorant and uncultured herd. After spending so many years mastering the subtleties of *katha-revousa*, they could hardly be expected to reject it. Trianda-phyllidis reports a conversation in 1909 with a teacher who justified teaching his pupils to write the *katharevousa opsarion* instead of the demotic *psari* ('fish' – note that the purist version is longer by three sounds) in terms of social respectability: 'We can't write *psari*: can we go out into the street with unkempt hair and dirty finger-nails? Well, it's the same with language' (Triandaphyllidis 1912: 300). On the contrary, it was the more cultivated members of the bourgeoisie who saw *katharevousa* as 'unaesthetic' and as a sign of vulgar pretension.

In the early nineteenth century it was axiomatic that the differences between Modern and Ancient Greek were the result not of gradual and inevitable development over two millennia, but of a national barbarization resulting from Turkish rule; since this barbarization had taken place in a mere four centuries, the argument went, it could be reversed in a few generations. It was Korais who first talked syste-matically about the need to 'correct' Modern Greek according to Ancient Greek rules, and to describe every formal difference between the two languages as a 'corruption' and every difference in meaning of a word as a 'misuse'.[3] So much 'correction' had taken place by the end of the century that *katharevousa* had become an established institution that one questioned at one's peril.

The chief arguments used by the defenders of *katharevousa* in the late nineteenth and early twentieth centuries are

41

clearly laid out by Hadzidakis: '(a) that our written language, formed and preserved since long ago, is the necessary and natural product of the history of our language *(sic)*, which is exceptionally conservative, and of our ancient, perpetual, and unique civilization; (b) that neither this language, nor the archaic elements to be found in it, are dead [. . .]; (c) that it is absolutely impossible to throw [. . .] our written language into the sea and make another to replace it' (1907b: 8). This was the argument from the *status quo*; but there was also the argument that demotic was split into dialects and for that reason, among others, was inadequate for the official language of a nation state. In other European countries, the spoken language of a dominant group formed the basis for the national written language; but no group spoke *katharevousa*, which was (even by Hadzidakis) conceived of only as a *written* language. Naturally the very existence of a different written language, which deprived the spoken language of the opportunity of being developed for use in various areas of life, kept the spoken language in a state of comparative impoverishment. This impoverishment was then used as a (somewhat circular) argument against its use in writing. There was a (perhaps deliberate) confusion made between the *relative* inadequacy of demotic at a particular time and its alleged *inherent* lack of potential for being developed. The purists failed to distinguish between dialect on the one hand and style and use of language on the other. As early as 1893 Roidis pointed out the confusion in the purists' minds between language and style (modern socio-linguists would talk about 'register'): other nations have different *styles*, not different *languages* for written and spoken use (1913: 192–3). They also failed to acknowledge that 'there is no necessary connection between dialect and lexis. Vocabularies are open-ended, and it is possible to combine academic and scientific vocabulary with non-standard grammatical forms' (Trudgill 1983: 197). Thus Korais, who confined his researches almost exclusively to a study of *words* and was aware of the lack of demotic vocabulary for modern western European concepts, was not content to introduce new words into demotic; rather, along with the new words, he attempted to revive almost the entire ancient system of declensions and conjugations. Thus Hadzidakis, who had studied the Modern Greek dialects more deeply than anyone before him, accused the demoticists of trying to turn the clock back to the poetic and picturesque – but by now lexically inadequate – language of the folk songs by discarding all innovations that had enriched the written language during the previous century (1907b: 20–1).

As early as 1884, at the outset of his academic career, Hadzidakis had written that demotic could not be used for all purposes until it had been studied completely and in its entirety (1884: 82). This he proceeded to do with laudable application for the rest of his career; but a quarter of a century later his conclusions were that the spoken language was poor and split into mutually incomprehensible dialects (1907b: 41 and 51); indeed, just as other purists often described demotic as a 'patois' or 'jargon', so Hadzidakis consistently argued that the Greeks spoke only dialects, while *katharevousa* alone could be termed a language. Arguing that each demoticist writes in his own individual-language, he claimed to be arguing from the point of view of 'the entire nation', which likes *(sic)* the written language and has rejected Psycharis' 'heresy' (ibid., 59): he conveniently suppressed any notion that there could be a demotic refined by an admixture of *katharevousa* elements, which in the event is how the language subsequently developed.

One of the deleterious consequences of the purists' blindness to historical change was that, starting with Korais, they treated Modern Greek not as an autonomous language with its own grammatical system, but as an appendage of Ancient Greek, whose only virtue is that it contains vestiges of Ancient Greek that we might not otherwise know from the extant texts of antiquity. Hadzidakis too practised linguistic archaeology, sifting the Modern Greek dialects for ancient relics. In 1908 Professor G. Mistriotis wrote: 'There is no Modern Greek grammar, because our language has become assimilated to the ancient . . . If we create a new grammar, we shall have created a new nation.' In the same year P. Karolidis opined: 'A grammar of the Modern Greek language cannot exist. [. . . The difference between the ancient and the modern languages] is so small that there is no need for two grammars' (both quoted in Triandaphyllidis 1982: 109–10). One trouble with such statements is that one does not know if by 'grammar' the writer is referring to the implicit rules governing a language, irrespective of whether they have been codified and explicated by a grammarian, or to a grammar-book. Clearly it is impossible to discover the rules of a language which one does not see as an autonomous system; but since the Greeks have been used since time immemorial to learning Greek (i.e. Ancient Greek) from a grammar-book, the absence of such a book in the early days of demoticism seemed to prove that demotic was not a language. Hadzidakis repeatedly said that one could not teach demotic in schools – let alone introduce it as the official language – until it had been fully codified. Triandaphyllidis realized (as he said in a letter written in 1910) that *katharevousa* owed some of its prestige to the fact that it was based on pre-existing grammatical rules which were enshrined in grammar books (in fact, he was overestimating the uniformity of *katharevousa* in this respect): people asked where were the grammatical rules and books that demotic was based on, not realizing that grammatical rules are abstractions based on existing phenomena (Triandaphyllidis 1982: xxxii–xxxiii).

Korais and Hadzidakis asserted that diglossia was both natural and universal: that there was inevitably one language for the educated and another for the vulgar herd. Hadzidakis explicitly confined the uneducated to a *passive* participation in national culture: as far as he was concerned, it was enough that they should *understand* (or figure out by guesswork) what they were told, and it did not bother him whether they possessed an *active* competence in the written language (1907b: 27 and 37). Thus he divided the nation into the few who write and the many who read (and half-comprehend). The result of diglossia was to keep the masses of the people in subjection and to exclude them from access to power; but, worst of all, by forcing the Greeks from the earliest age to eradicate the most precious words in their vocabulary and to replace them with 'better words' (cf. Triandaphyllidis 1912: 283–4), it caused them to be ashamed of their own culture and ultimately alienated from themselves.

The rhetoric of purism is full of adjectives such as 'correct', 'rich', 'pure', 'noble', and even 'sacred' to describe Ancient Greek and/or *katharevousa*, and their antonyms 'ungrammatical', 'poor', 'corrupt' or 'adulterated', 'vulgar' or 'base', and 'profane' or even 'blasphemous' to refer to demotic. There is an even richer rhetoric of demoticism to refer to the different forms of Greek. The demoticists followed

44

Herder and Humbold in their belief that a language expresses the soul of the people that speaks it (Tziovas 1985: 274-5). The demoticist view of language was that it was a dynamic, living organism created by the people, while *katharevousa* was the 'construct' of an unrepresentative clique. While the purists accepted as inevitable the divisions between the cultural élite and the rest of the people, the nationalist demoticists dreamed of a unified, homogeneous nation. Whereas the purists favoured writing as more permanent and authoritative, the demoticists promoted speech as being genuine, natural, immediate, and authentic, and as springing directly from the soul (Tziovas 1986: 232-3 and *passim*).

The demoticists constantly claimed that their struggle was for truth and reality (though not to the exclusion of the ideal) against falsehood and pipe-dreams. They called for liberation and enlightenment as opposed to bondage and obscurantism, creativity and originality rather than sterility and imitation (vegetating in the shade of Ancient Greece). They promoted the feeling heart over the reasoning intellect, 'the spirit that giveth life' over 'the letter that killeth' (II Cor. 3:5, quoted by Triandaphyllidis 1982: 79). They were orientated more towards nature and to rural life than to artifice and urban values: indeed, the demoticists tended to ignore the urban proletariat in favour of the agricultural population. They supported poetry against pedantry, simplicity against complexity, freshness against dryness, and pounding blood against crumbling bones. Their writings are full of images of dawn, hope for the future, joy and life, and they associate purism with twilight, nostalgia for the past, sorrow, and death. But most of all they stress the primacy of speech, of one's native tongue, against the secondary process of writing, especially when that writing is done in what is more or less a foreign language, which opens an additional chasm between the writer and the object or concept about which he is writing.

Nevertheless, the demoticists were often just as guilty as the purists of demanding an impossible ideal and of promoting an artificial version of Modern Greek. Psycharis was the first demoticist to polarize demotic and *katharevousa* by opposing any *rapprochement* between the two, and by doing so provided his opponents with valuable ammunition. Psycharis' view (attacked by Hadzidakis) was that demotic should consist of a pristine language stripped of any *katharevousa* encrustations; he based his argument on 'the unchangeable laws of historical linguistics', and set aside any contributions that the purists may have made to the Modern Greek vocabulary, insisting instead on creating new words, according to demotic rules, for the various concepts that were lacking from the spoken language of the uneducated. Psycharis asserted that there should be one unified language, and that poets were not permitted to depart from the usage of ordinary people. This enabled purists such as Angelos Vlachos to condemn the demotic employed by poets as a cryptographic code, incomprehensible to either educated or uneducated Greeks (Vlachos 1891: 283), and Hadzidakis to allege repeatedly that the demotic of the demoticists 'has never been spoken'.

A consequence of this polarization was the constantly expressed desire even of the less intransigent demoticists of the Educational Society for a linguistic uniformity and homogeneity. All too often demoticists have attempted to ostracize words that are commonly used in everyday speech even by uneducated people, on the grounds that their inflection does not conform with demotic rules; thus, like the purists, they have tried to jettison half the language, confining it, in their case, to simplistic — or, at best, poetic — use.

The demoticists always insisted that demotic is not a dialect, but consists of the common elements of the spoken language, free of regionalisms. The description given by Triandaphyllidis in 1926 of the version of Greek that he promoted is worth quoting (the italics are mine): 'I believe that our common language must be founded on *the language of our people*, on *its common form*, according to the *pan-Hellenic sense* of the living langauge and *the form that has been developed in our folk songs* and cultivated in our literature, without archaic and *regional* features.' He goes on to explain that the 'common form' is that which has been spoken in those 'linguistic centres' of the Peloponnese and Sterea Ellas (i.e. the southern mainland) which have determined the common language spoken in the cities today, with some *katharevousa* additions. The 'pan-Hellenic linguistic sense' is manifested in the way in which the majority of the people make new words conform with demotic linguistic rules, and this common form of the language is that which has been cultivated in literature (Triandaphyllidis 1982: 116). Apart from the weakness of his evidence for his postulated 'pan-Hellenic linguistic sense' and his failure to define 'regional' (is Athenian or Salonican usage 'regional'?), he omits any comment on his reference to the language of the folk songs. I would like to dwell on this, because Trianda-phyllidis and other demoticists have been fond of invoking the folk songs in support of their view that there was already a 'common' form of Modern Greek before they invented it; in his grammar of 1941 (as in Tzartzanos' standard syntax of 1946–63) a huge number of examples illustrative of grammatical phenomena have been taken from the folk songs. The grammarians of demotic failed to realize (or acknowledge) the way in which folk songs were traditionally edited by Greek scholars, who tended to strip them of dialectal features. The prime example is N. G. Politis, whose standard *Selections from the Songs of the Greek People* (1914), taught in Greek schools for decades, consists not of songs as they were actually sung, but of 'reconstructions' of what the editor believed to be the 'original texts', of which the actual performances were often imperfect recollections. Politis created the impression (and one that is still prevalent in Greece) that the Greek folk had, in their songs, forged a common language free of dialectalisms – that is, nothing less than a standardized literary language. This misunderstanding was a powerful weapon in the demoticists' hands; but, as urbanization has proceeded in recent years and rural values have come to be seen as out of date, many Greeks have turned against the demotic of the demoticists precisely because of its 'folksy' connotations.

One of the failures of the Educational Society as the mouthpiece of the demoticist movement was that it confined the language question to the sphere of education (and to primary education at that), and that it limited educational reform to altering the language of school textbooks without reforming their content. All too often the arguments about the language have centred around disputes about the relative teachability of the various versions of Modern Greek. I some-times suspect that the fact that the same adjective *(dimotiko)* is used in Greek for 'demotic' language, 'primary' school, and 'folk' songs may have caused such a deep-rooted confusion in people's minds that these three concepts are seen as being inextricably interlinked. Ever since the language controversy began, schools — and particularly primary schools — have been seen as nurseries of the national language, and the language used in school textbooks has always been subject to scrutiny, since it has been seen as reflecting the state's language policy at any particular time. This is why the language of school textbooks has tended to change with each change of government. It has also been a widespread view that Greek children should be taught the rules of Greek grammar from an ideally infallible grammar-book provided by the state. Thus Triandaphyllidis' monumental 'state grammar' of 1941, and the abridgements of it made since for school use, have inevitably been subject to criticism on points of principle and detail whenever the particular critic finds that the proportion of *katharevousa* features incorporated into the grammar is either too small or too great for his liking. Now, almost fifty years after the publication of the original grammar, voices are often raised calling for a completely new Modern Greek grammar to be compiled which will exactly represent the Greek spoken by educated urban Greeks, while others argue either for the preservation of Triandaphyllidis or even for a complete eradication of *katharevousa* influences. Thus the demoticists' obsession with the language of education has caused the language question to be bogged down in sterile debates on minute details of primary-school language rather than allowing the debate to open out into the wider aspects of language use.

What, then, are the consequences of *katharevousa*? First of all, it divided the Greek nation into those who possessed and those who did not possess the magic words that ensured them social and economic success. But there are other consequences. Adamandios Pepelasis, Governor of the Agricultural Bank of Greece, said in 1977: 'The lack of communication and mutual understanding between education, science, and scholarship on the one hand, and the people on the other has kept the latter in ignorance and made the former sterile and unproductive': the people have been hindered from access to scientific knowledge and the rationalization of reality (*Provlimata* 1977: 120). Because it is a language that has to be laboriously learned, *katharevousa* has brought about a pedantic literalness and a fear of figurative language in the writings of those who have been brought up with it. On the other hand, because there has never been any agreed norm for *katharevousa* — since it is an arbitrary mixture of two languages, Ancient and Modern Greek — the sense that 'with Kath[arevousa], anything goes' (Petrounias 1978: 205) has been extended to demotic too, with a consequent linguistic anarchy in usage that Metaxas has been far from the only Greek to bewail. It has also brought about an unfortunate linguistic uncertainty and insecurity among Greeks whenever they come to write: how can they write 'correctly'? how will they avoid being ridiculed for their 'mistakes'? It has often led to such a concentration on form that content has been all but ignored; vacuous and pretentious pomposity is an almost indispensible hallmark of writing in *katharevousa*, and this has often been transferred to writing in demotic.

Perhaps the only aspect of the language that has benefited from the attentions of the purists is the vocabulary. Although a large number of 'zombie-words' were revived from Ancient Greek, or coined on Ancient Greek models, in the nineteenth century when there were perfectly good demotic words already for the same concepts, there is no doubt that where demotic words did not exist, the purists often carried out a very successful operation in filling the gaps with ingenious revivals or coinages, most of which survive today, and many have become such everyday words in speech that hardly any Greek is aware that they were artificially inseminated into the language by purists only a century or so ago. Although such coining could equally well have been carried out had demotic been adopted for official purposes in 1821, nevertheless *katharevousa* has been at least partially vindicated in the remarkable number of its neologisms that have incorporated themselves into the language (cf. Andriotis 1976: 317).

'Do you think I have anything in mind but liberty and language?' asked the poet Solomos in 1824, during the War of Independence, which he believed was a struggle to liberate the Greeks from the dual tyranny of the Turks and the pedants. In the event, the second part of the struggle was not completed until precisely one and a half centuries later. The Greeks' struggle for independence, not only from the Turks but also from the various 'protecting powers', was accompanied, from the days of Solomos onwards, by a struggle for the official recognition of Greek popular culture.

Ironically, by the time this battle was won, that popular culture itself had all but disappeared. The language controversy looks now to have been something of an anachronism and a diversion, and the Greeks today are struggling to form and preserve a cultural, social, economic, and political identity amid the crushingly powerful claims on their attention from all quarters – Europe, America, Asia, and elsewhere.

NOTES

1 It is impossible for linguists to agree on the degree of closeness of Modern Greek to Ancient Greek, since their pronouncements inevitably reflect their point of view. Thus Hadzidakis argued that it was the morphological similarities that bore the most persuasive witness to the closeness of the two languages (1907b: 25-6), while Householder writes that of the features distinguishing demotic from *katharevousa* (and *a fortiori* from Ancient Greek), inflection is the most important (1962: 122).

2 The word *yenos* ('race') is used here, as so often at the time, to refer to Greeks throughout the Greek-speaking world (Macedonia, Asia Minor, and elsewhere), and not just within the Greek state.

3 Korais' fetish for the written word (shared by most other purists, and even by the arch-demoticist Psycharis) is aptly illustrated by his proposal, made in 1807, that the Ecumenical Patriarch and the Synod of the Greek Church (which were at that time the only existing Greek authorities) should forbid ancient manuscripts to be taken out of Greece and should establish a Greek Museum containing manuscripts, coins, and any pots, stones, columns, etc., *bearing inscriptions*, and such other remains of Greek art and history *(sic)* as may be found (1984: 256-8). His insistence on inscriptions shows that for him it was words rather than objects that bore witness to the past; and it is indicative that he makes no mention of the Parthenon marbles, which Lord Elgin had by then shipped to Britain.

BIBLIOGRAPHY

Alexiou, M. (1982). 'Diglossia in Greece', in W. Haas (ed.), *Standard Languages, Spoken and Written*, Manchester, pp. 156–92.

Andriotis, N. P. (1967). *Etymologiko lexiko tis kinis neoellinikis*. Salonica. [1st ed. 1951].

—— (1976). *Andicharisma ston kathigiti N. P. Andrioti*. Salonica.

Bien, P. (1972). *Kazantzakis and the Linguishi Revolution in Greek Literature*. Princeton.

Browning, R. (1983). *Medieval and Modern Greek*. 2nd ed. Cambridge.

Christidis, Ch. (1974). *Politiki dikonomia 1971. Dokimio metagrafis tis stin ethniki glossa ton Ellinon*. Athens.

Dimaras, A. (1974). *I metarrythmisi pou den egine*. Vol. 2. Athens.

Etairia (1905). *I Etairia 'I Ethniki Glossa' pros to elliniko ethnos*. Athens.

Hadzidakis, G. N. (1884). *Meleti epi tis neas ellinikis*. Athens. (1907a). *Kai palin peri tou glossikou zitimatos*. Athens. [Greek version of the following]

—— (1907b). *La Question de la langue écrite néo-grecque*. Athens.

Householder, F. W. (1962). 'Greek diglossia', *Georgetown Monographs* 15, pp. 109–32.

Kondos, K. S. (1882). *Glossike paratirisis anaferomene is tin Nean Ellinikin*

Glossan. Athens.

Konemenos, N. (1873). *To zitima tis glossas.* Corfu.

Korais, A. (1984). *Prolegomena stous archeous Ellines syngrafis.* Athens.

Mackridge, P. (1985). *The Modern Greek Language.* Oxford.

Mirambel, A. (1937). 'Les "Etats de langue" dans la Grèce actuelle'. *Conférences de l'Institut linguistique de l'Université de Paris*, V, pp. 19-53.

───── (1964). 'Les aspects psychologiques du purisme dans la Grèce moderne'. *Journal de psychologie normale at pathologique*, no. 4, pp. 405-36.

Moschonas, E. (1975). 'Enas eonas dimotikismou. Kinonikes ke politikes prosengisis', in A. Pallis, *Brousos*, Athens, pp. xii–cxxi.

Petrounias, E. (1978). 'The Modern Greek language and diglossia', in S. Vryonis (ed.), *The 'Past' in Modern Greek Culture*, Malibu, pp. 193-220.

Politis, N. G. (1914). *Ekloge apo ta tragoudia tou ellinikou laou.* Athens.

Provlimata (1977). *Provlimata metaglottismou sti neoelliniki glossa.* Athens.

Psycharis, Y. (1971). *To taxidi mou.* Athens, [1st ed., 1888].

Roidis, E. (1913). *Ta idola.* Athens, [1st ed., 1893].

Rorty, R. (1986). 'The Contingency of Language', *London Review of Books*, 17 April 1986.

Skliros, G. (1907). *To kinonikon mas zitima.* Athens.

Soutsos, P. (1853). *I Nea Scholi tou grafomenou logou.* Athens.

Stavridi-Patrikiou, R. (ed.) (1976). *Dimotikismos ke kinoniko provlima.* Athens.

Toynbee, A. (1981). 'The Greek Language's Vicissitudes in the Modern Age', in *The Greeks and their Heritages*, Oxford, pp. 245-67.

Triandaphyllidis, M. (1912). 'I pedia mas ke i glossa tis'. *Deltio tou Ekpedeftikou Omilou*, 2, pp. 271-309.

───── (1941). *Neoelliniki grammatiki (tis Dimotikis).* Athens.

───── (1982). *Epilogi apo to ergo tou.* Salonica.

Trudgill, P. (1983). *On Dialect.* Oxford.

Tzartzanos, A. (1946-63). *Neoelliniki syntaxis (tis kinis dimotikis).* Athens, [1st ed., 1928].

Tziovas, D. (1986). *The Nationism of the Demoticists and its Impact on their Literary Theory (1888-1930).* Amsterdam.

───── (1985). 'The organic discourse of nationistic demoticism: a tropological approach', in M. Alexiou and V. Lambropoulos (eds.), *The Text and its Margins: Post-Structuralist Approaches to Twentieth-Century Greek Literature*, New York, pp. 253-77.

[Vernardakis, D.] (1884). *Psevdattikismou elenchos, iti K. S. Kondou Glossikon paratiriseon [. . .] anaskevi.* Trieste.

Vlachos, A. (1891). 'Filadelfios piitikos agon: Ekthesis tis epitropis ton agonodikon'. *Estia*, July-December 1891, pp. 281-8.

THE GREEK ECONOMY

Jon Kofas

The Truman Declaration of March 1947 by which the US took over Britain's role as 'protecting power' in Greece raised the immediate prospect of American economic aid.

A. Conditions for United States Aid to Greece

The Maximos Government, the right wing elements and the business community in Greece were euphoric about the new era of Greek dependence on the United States. For many in the armed forces, the bureaucracy, the business community and in politics the Truman Doctrine signified that Greece's fate was inexorably linked with the West and would not be abandoned by the latter. The initial optimism, however, evaporated quickly when the price of American assistance became fully known.

The Porter Mission conferred with Premier Maximos and the Currency Committee on 21 March and submitted a number of proposals to Washington and Athens concerning Greek economic and fiscal policy. The most important recommendation revolved around the need for rigorous trade controls under the authority of a centralized Foreign Trade Administration which the Americans eventually controlled. Second, the United States officials insisted that foreign exchange and gold sales by the central bank must be curtailed for they had detrimental effects on the economy. It should be noted that gold sales ceased entirely after 12 March 1947 and the currency was relatively stable for a few months until gold sales resumed. Finally, Porter urged the Hellenic government to impose strict price/wage controls as one plausible method of controlling rampant inflation.

Porter underscored the need for a permanent American mission which would be authorized to postpone or withdraw aid and 'exercise general supervision and participate in the development of fiscal policy'. Moreover, the mission would also supervise surplus property, Export–Import Bank loans to Greece, and private as well as governmental imports. Prime Minister Maximos agreed to comply with Porter's recommendations which were fully implemented after July 1947 once Marshall approved them. The Secretary of State insisted that American officials must control the Foreign Trade Administration and he requested that the government in Athens publicly acknowledge America's generosity as manifested in the Truman Doctrine.[1]

The Agreement on Greek Aid was signed on 31 May by the government in Athens, thereby formally designating the beginning of *Americanokratia*. The Agreement was drafted by American officials and submitted to Greek officials for their approval. It subjected the country to unprecedented controls because the twelve articles of the Agreement granted AMAG virtually limitless authority over all facets of government. Article VI was the key to AMAG's comprehensive military and economic functions in Greece. It stated that:

> The Govt of Greece will permit the members of the American Mission to observe freely the utilization of assistance furnished to Greece by the U.S. The Govt of Greece will maintain such accounts and records, will furnish the American Mission such reports and information, as the Mission may request for the performance of its function and responsibilities.[2]

The Agreement permitted AMAG to control the organs of the state, which was a flagrant violation of the nation's sovereignty. Such was the price, however, that the regime reluctantly paid to sustain itself in power and preserve the *status quo* which the Democratic Army threatened.

Every social sector was thoroughly permeated by the ubiquitous influence of the American mission. Professor William McNeill, who approved of foreign aid as part of the solution for Greece's complex problems, described AMAG's infiltration of Greece as follows:

Advisers had been installed in the Ministries, field representatives had been stationed all over the country to check upon actual performance and when things went wrong or failed to conform to American ideas, vigorous efforts were made to alter the situation through 'advice' that often took on a peremptory tone.[3]

Initially, American ascendancy in Greece was confined to military and financial matters, but gradually every sector, from labour to education, was affected.

The Agreement on Greek Aid extended such comprehensive powers to AMAG that it had the effect of rendering the host government 'unable to take any important decision without their (AMAG) approval'.

B. Protracted Economic Dislocation, Refugees and Guerrillas

When the American mission arrived in Greece, the government's most immediate problem was the depleted finances. The central bank's gold stock stood at $4 million, the dollar reserves amounted to a mere $150,000, excluding currency cover of $3,000,000, and the sterling reserves were down to $3,500,000, also excluding currency cover. All dollar-import applications were denied because of the bank's precarious position. The Attlee Government extended a $2 million loan to Greece as cover for the foreign exchange requirements in April 1947, but that was not sufficient to counterpoise further financial debasement.[4]

In spring 1947 there was a maritime strike which had a crippling effect on the country's food imports and other essentials such as fuel. The labour strike coincided with the suspension of UNRRA operations. The United States Embassy informed the State Department that Greece was facing an imminent danger of famine and disease with cataclysmic consequences for the prospects of economic recovery.

A principal factor in the low productivity rate in Greece was that about 30 percent of all manpower was engaged either in the military and the gendarmerie, or was part of an ever-expanding refugee population. Colonel A. W. Sheppard argued in his study of post-war Greece that between 1945 and 1947, the period of considerable foreign assistance and British intervention, unemployment jumped 11 percent in the urban sector, the drachma devalued from 600 to 20,000 per pound sterling, and the cost of living soared 34 percent between March 1945 and December 1946. The national income in 1947 was 62.6 percent of the pre-war level and the per capita income was 59.6 percent of the pre-war level. The average income per head was $52.8 annually in 1947 as compared to $90 in 1938, measured in 1938 value. Clearly, therefore, foreign aid and advice between the Athens Revolt and the Truman Doctrine had exacerbated, not alleviated Greece's problems. Again, this is not to say that aid *per se* was responsible for the above-mentioned conditions. Its application, however, under Greece's political economy in the late 1940s accounted for its negative results.[5]

Ambassador MacVeagh suggested to the authorities in Athens in June 1947 that they needed to purchase $500,000 in petroleum products to meet the immediate civil and defence needs. Furthermore, the government purchased $2 million in food supplies to avert a food shortage crisis, but the Treasury lacked the funds for other extensive essential imports. The United States Embassy estimated that Greece's balance of payments deficit would rise to $8.4 million if the most essential supplies were purchased for the month of July only.

C. AMAG's Preeminence and the Failure of Foreign Aid

The Greek government knew that AMAG would have pre-eminent control of Greek affairs. What was not known, however, was the degree of the Mission's powers and the effects of its policies on the country's economy and finances. When AMAG formally commenced operations in the middle of July, it was organized into a number of departments attached to the Greek ministries and public agencies. American experts on the Mission included military officers, agronomists, engineers, industrial technicians, experts in the areas of finance, welfare, transportation and labour relations.

AMAG placed under its supervision all branches of the Greek government and gave priority to the armed forces. One State Department memo ascertained that:

> Its (AMAG's) advisory services cover all segments of the Greek economy, including such matters as governmental administration and procedure, internal budgetary and fiscal controls, control of all foreign exchange resources, programming and control of imports. . .[6]

The Mission was in a paramount position to exert all-embracing influence in Greek affairs because the Aid Agreement allowed for American officials to dominate the Currency Committee, the Foreign Trade Administration and the Central Loan Committee; all vital networks in setting monetary, fiscal and commercial policies.

The Counterpart Account was one of AMAG's most powerful tools in determining the financial policy of Greece. The drachmas derived from the sale of goods under the aid programme were deposited in a special fund at the Bank of Greece. The Mission had jurisdiction over those funds which were initially designated for reconstruction and economic development projects. Eventually, the Counterpart funds were absorbed by the immense budget deficits or they were blocked by AMAG in an attempt to halt inflation. C. A. Munkman, former UNRRA and AMAG official, has written that the Americans used the Counterpart Account to manipulate Greek financial policy. He stated that:

> The policy of the government and of the Bank of Greece in turn was completely subordinated to the actions taken by the American Mission in making essential imports available to the economy . . . However, apart from the policy control (enjoyed by the Currency Committee) the American Mission, through the counterpart account was by far the largest depositor with the Bank of Greece and consequently was able to influence the credit situation by manipulation of this account.[7]

The Greek banking system was divided into agricultural and commercial banks whose function was to extend credit to the private sector. With the exception of the National Bank, the other banks had only limited deposits after the war. Thus they relied on the Bank of Greece for funds. The central bank was the state's official agent and its most important function in the 1940s was to extend credit to the government to cover the budget deficits.

The first shipments of American assistance arrived belatedly in August 1947, just as the State Department conveyed serious doubts concerning the prospects of an early recovery in Greece. Congress approved the Greek–Turkish Aid Bill with the understanding that the programme would end in June 1948; there was no mention of a permanent United States presence in Greece. The State Department argued in August 1947 that 'accomplishment of our economic objectives would be difficult under any circumstances, and continuation of adverse conditions in all important security and political fields will make their attainment impossible.'[8]

The monumental task of reconstruction was indeed impossible in just a year's time, especially considering that military aid absorbed most of the funds earmarked for economic aid. Such reallocation of funds was carried out by AMAG with the recognition that Greece suffered immense wheat and other foodstuff deficits in summer 1947. Moreover, the Mission restricted imports and tightened monetary policy in order to curb inflation. Such deflationary policies had an adverse effect on the economy as was to be expected. Finally, the enunciation of the Truman Doctrine and the aid accompanying it had an ephemeral impact on the Greek business community. Neither the businessmen nor the politicians believed that a mere $300 million was sufficient to secure long term monetary stability, especially since most of the funds were spent for defence. As a result of this lack of confidence, inflation was running at the rate of 50 percent annually and currency circulation increased from 537 billion drachmas in 1946 to 970 billions in 1947, indicative of the continuing trend of devaluation. Moreover, there were 100,000 unemployed workers in Athens alone with no immediate prospects of finding work. Finally, the cost of living index in the capital soared from 145.2 in 1946 to 174.6 in 1947.

The precipitous rise in defence expenditures after March 1947 resulted in greater budget deficits which were in turn covered by funds that could have been devoted to economic revitalization. This process obviously prolonged economic dislocation. Reconstruction appropriations in fiscal year 1946–1947 were less than one-tenth of military and public security appropriations. In the same fiscal year 35 percent of the budget was incorporated into the ministries of Army, Navy, Air Force and Public Security. The central bank advanced 510 billion drachmas to the state in 1946 to cover the deficit and 882 billions ($176.4 million) in 1947. Given the state's immense defence expenditures and the regressive tax structure, the prospects of a speedy economic recovery analogous to that of Yugoslavia and most of the other North Balkan countries was unlikely in Greece.[9]

The American Mission for Aid to Greece accomplished

very little in stimulating the civilian economy because it concentrated its efforts on the more exigent military problems. Consequently, agricultural production was 85.2 percent of the prewar (1938) level and industrial production was 67 percent of the 1939 level. There was a direct correlation between the low productivity rates and the incessant rise in the cost of living. The cost of living index jumped from 20,473 in August 1947 to 23,047 in November. The central bank's reserves had dwindled even further, reaching $5 million in September 1947. AMAG, therefore, had not inspired confidence in the economy as was expected and its policy advice had not yielded any positive results.

The Greek government informed the Mission in November that $46 million of the $55 million of Greece's surplus property in the United States had been used and the remaining $9 million was intended to cover future purchases. The Truman administration planned to allocate an additional $40 million to Greece for foodstuffs as conditions in the country degenerated further with the rise of the refugee population. Griswold maintained that increased economic and military assistance to Greece was necessary not only for strategic, but also for political considerations. Governor Griswold and Loy Henderson had become personally entangled in the formation of a new coalition Government in which the centrists, headed by Sofoulis and the rightists led by Tsaldaris shared power. More aid was imperative to give the Americans in Athens greater leverage with the precarious centre-right coalition.[10]

The AMAG chief requested an additional $15.3 million in economic aid because import prices in foreign exchange had increased 10 percent since April 1947. He also asked for $50 million in relief costs for fiscal year 1947–1948. The refugee problem was politically sensitive for obvious reasons and the Mission pointed to it as one of the pernicious consequences of the Civil War. The cost of the refugees to the state was enormous and, according to the American Consulate in Thessaloniki, it constituted a major drain on the Treasury. The Consulate's report stated that:

> The Greek Government has been spending recently 8.4 billion drachmas monthly for the care of displaced persons, equivalent to $1,680,000 at the rate of 5,000 drachmas to the dollar. For the care of 284,812 needy displaced persons from October 1, 1947

through June 30, 1948 the Greek Government has estimated that it will require 241,415 billion drachmas, the equivalent of \$48,283,000.[11]

The American Mission concluded in November 1947 that unless the military situation improved in favour of the National Army, the refugee problem 'will assume proportions as to threaten the national economy and stability of the government'.

The National Army was strengthened after November 1947, but the rebels were difficult to subdue, as is often the case in guerrilla warfare, partly because they enjoyed the assistance of the peasants and Greece's Balkan neighbours. Meanwhile, the civilian population was indignant toward the regime because the Civil War took precedence over economic problems. The American Foreign Relief programme reached the following conclusions in its Second Report to Congress.

In addition to the 430,000 refugees, the Ministry of Welfare, in November 1947, reported that 1,617,132 persons were certified as indigent, yet of this number only 1,124,179 persons, substantially half a million fewer persons, were entitled to receive free rations. Only those indigents in communities less than 3,000 received supplies free. Persons were defined as indigent if they had a monthly income of \$6.25 in some localities to \$15 in others.[12]

Despite the inability of foreign relief and aid programmes to redress such ominous conditions in Greece, Griswold believed in the efficacy of aid and went so far as to claim that AMAG had a record of numerous accomplishments. He ascertained that construction was started on 1,647.1 kilometres of highway; on the Corinth Canal and the harbours of Thessaloniki; on two major railways (Brallo Tunnel and Gorgopotamos Bridge) and on five major air fields; all under the auspices of the Americans.

The rebuilding of the basic infrastructure was certainly an important part of the overall reconstruction process and its value should not be underestimated. The construction projects which were undertaken under AMAG's auspices, however, were concentrated in northern Greece — the core of the Democratic Army's operations — and in the capital due to political and strategic considerations rather than economic. AMAG-sponsored projects, therefore, were mostly military-related and practically all economic aid under Public Law 87 was devoted to such projects. From a total of $350 million, which Greece received in American aid during fiscal 1947–1948, $82 million was expended on the rebuilding of the military-related infrastructure, while the rest went directly to defence and administrative expenses.

The Mission's most serious shortcoming, by its own admission, was in the housing sector. An AMAG report stated that: 'The housing programme exclusive of the provisions of refugee shelter, calls for the reconstruction of a total of 12,500 units by June 30 (1948). As of February 29, 3,620 units had been completed.' AMAG claimed favourable results as pertaining to refugee housing. Under its programme, there were 1,381 temporary huts built and 6,250 rooms in war-damaged buildings which housed 6,404 families. The number of refugees, however, exceeded 500,000 by spring 1948 and the Mission's programme had not provided but for a fraction of that population.

AMAG's annual report (1948) maintained that the Mission would revive the Greek industrial and agricultural production to surpass the pre-war levels; that it would assist in the stimulation of exports, while helping to reduce the nation's dependence on imports; that it would eliminate the wasteful and cumbersome bureaucracy; that it would strive toward a balanced budget, stabilize the currency and strengthen the national economy. Every year that passed since that unduly optimistic report was compiled, the size of the government bureaucracy – the product of political patronage – increased, budget deficits burgeoned, the public debt soared, the economy was dominated by foreign capital and Greece left more dependent on the advanced capitalist countries.[13]

The Greeks remained largely unconvinced by the Mission's promises and optimistic outlook on the economy. Both the liberal and conservative press disapproved of AMAG policies, though for different reasons. Spyros Markezinis, an ultra-conservative politician, charged that Washington did not provide sufficient assistance, particularly military, for Greece. He and others in the rightist camp assailed Greek officials who followed blindly the advice of the Americans regardless of the soundness of that advice. They argued that if the coalition Government was unable to convince foreign advisers of their policy errors, then the entire Cabinet must resign. A deep sense of nationalism coupled with the disillusionment of foreign aid prompted the conservatives to criticize AMAG policies.

Much of the criticism levelled against the Mission was also due to the overbearing role of Governor Griswold in Greek politics. In October 1947 he approved sweeping tax increases which some conservatives opposed. One newspaper, *Nea Alitheia*, charged that United States officials and the Sofoulis/Tsaldaris administration did not have the 'power to hit the pockets of the mighty and privileged, (in approving Griswold's tax reform plan) so they found easy recourse of making up the deficit' by burdening the poor with additional consumption taxes.[14]

One critic, who had originally supported the Truman Doctrine, published the following article on 31 October 1947, denouncing Griswold's shortsightedness regarding fiscal policy.

> The complete disclosure of the inadequacy of the aid voted and of the ineffective handling has been brought about by the insistence of the American Mission to cover regular and extra public expenses by the pitiless indirect taxation, which necessarily pushes prices upward, i.e. it leads straight to monetary inflation, and salaries will have to follow the rising cost of living. The 150 percent increase announced in custom duties, on the very day when 23 countries which met in Geneva under the United States' leadership signed 123 trade agreements (General Agreement on Tariffs and Trade, GATT) which inaugurate the world-wide American endeavor to obtain a lowering of import duties, is particularly unbelievable, as it will cause the already high Greek prices to soar even higher. It would have been infinitely better to have left the state budget unbalanced. The Greek public would have believed blindly in an American promise that aid would be continued in the future.[15]

The above article reflected the sentiments of many Greek capitalists and conservatives in the political arena who were opposed to any tax increases. It is interesting to note that the State Department urged Latin American countries during the late 1940s to remove trade barriers and accept the General Agreement on Tariffs and Trade (GATT) principles. Greece's case was so desperate, however, that even the *laissez-faire*-minded Americans realized that the state needed to be strengthened if it was to survive at all. The criticism expressed in the above article had some merit because the Mission approved astronomical tax increases on essentials, while leaving luxury items and income taxes untouched. That was indeed an irresponsible measure for it accentuated hyper-inflation after October 1947.

Considering AMAG's shortcomings in economic and financial matters, liberal political circles in Greece began casting doubts about the Americans' role in the country. The liberals argued that a stringent monetary policy, combined with higher indirect taxes which affected the lower classes retarded economic growth. By the end of 1947, therefore, there was only a small minority that gave tacit approval to the American Mission's accomplishments in the country. In addition to the dissatisfaction with AMAG's policies, there was considerable resentment in the political arena and the bureaucracy toward Griswold whom many considered a pretentious authoritarian. The pugnacious Governor was a controversial figure because he was entrusted with comprehensive powers that left him in the prominent position of determining policy. The *New York Times* characterized him as 'The Most Powerful Man in Greece' in a complimentary feature story published on 12 October 1947. The article depicted the Governor as diligent, pertinacious, and flamboyant. It emphasized that there was hardly a major decision made in Greece without his approval.

Griswold was characteristically candid about his Mission's paramount influence in Greece and about the United States' role in that country's affairs. 'It is my considered opinion,' he wrote, 'that it would be wrong for AMAG or for the US Government to attempt to present to world opinion that AMAG does not have great power or that it is not involved in Greek internal affairs.' He went on to justify his Mission's exorbitant powers on the basis of endeavouring to administer American aid to Greece successfully. He denied, however, that he and his staff enjoyed 'unlimited authority' as the press alleged.[16]

Secretary Marshall generally concurred with Griswold's line of reasoning, but he deplored press criticism of United States foreign policy in Greece. 'While we agree it is necessary US influence and control over funds be recognized in Greece', he noted, 'we hope this can be accomplished through direct contacts of proper officials with Greek authorities and doubt that articles in American press are useful in this respect.' He warned that Western press reports alleging that America 'had taken over Greece' were more injurious to the Administration's foreign policy than any Soviet or Communist propaganda.[17]

One year of AMAG policy directives and economic development initiatives left the United States with a preponderant role in Greek affairs, but did not result in better conditions for the people or for the national economy. Under AMAG there was no long term reconstruction programme; there was continued financial bankruptcy and the value of the currency plummeted; the capitalist class continued to invest in gold and dollars; the refugee problem was exacerbated and life for the masses deteriorated. American aid to Greece under AMAG had few constructive aspects for it was designed to offer a military solution to a political problem which was caused by economic factors, social injustice and an unrepresentative and brutal regime. The most noteworthy achievement of AMAG was that it laid the foundations for American ascendancy in Greece.

D. Greece Under the Marshall Plan

The Marshall Plan was adopted in Greece when the Greek–American Economic Co-operation Agreement was signed on 2 July 1948. The AMAG relinquished its functions to the ECA/G which was accountable to the Paris-based ECA. The American Mission was reorganized and its functions centralized under the authority of Ambassador Henry F. Grady who assumed MacVeagh's and Griswold's duties.

One of the principal objectives of the ERP was to stimulate European exports and raise foreign exchange so that the balance of payments deficits would be eradicated or at least reduced. While that goal was largely achieved by 1951 in most European countries — the United Kingdom and Italy suffered notable trade deficits under the ERP — Greece lagged far behind Western Europe in almost every sector and it had the lowest standard of living in Europe. Greece's trade deficit amounted to $1,199,651,000 between 1948 and 1951; indicative of the dismal failure of foreign aid as a stimulus to an underdeveloped economy. The United States, which was Greece's principal trading partner, imported an average of 16.9 percent of Greek exports under the ERP, while during the same four-year period Greece imported an annual average of 36.6 percent of its aggregate imports from the United States. Since American officials were responsible for the direction of Greece's foreign trade, they obstructed the country from pursuing a multi-lateral foreign trade policy that would have served its best interests.[18]

Legislative Decree No. 588 was one of the legal devices which the American Mission used to apportion considerable authority to itself under ECA/G. Under that law, the Currency Committee determined the procedure and supervision of all credit allocation. The state was ultimately responsible for formulating credit policy, but the state was acting under the advice of the American agencies in Athens. Charles Coombs, AMAG financial expert and former Currency Committee member, devised Law 588. The object of that law was to centralize the nation's credit network, so that the United States Mission would be in the propitious position to implement a financial programme more efficaciously and without becoming exposed to public scrutiny.

The law required the National Bank of Greece to deposit 15 percent of its total deposits with the central bank. The other commercial banks were obliged to deposit 5 percent with the Bank of Greece. The National Bank had 263 billion drachmas, or 75 percent of the total deposits of public organizations. The United States Embassy argued that the National Bank 'has won an incomparable position in the Greek banking system and is seriously handicapping other commercial banks'. The National Bank had 346 billion of the total 506 billion drachmas of the aggregate banking capital in October 1948. Because of its monopolistic position and due to the restructuring of the banking system under the aegis of the Americans, the National Bank was compelled to strengthen the central bank whose policy was determined by the Mission.

There were many nuances to Law No. 588, some of which warrant further elucidation since they affected the country's economy. First, the Mission wanted to immobilize a sizeable sum of the bank deposits in order to create a deflationary effect in the economy. That was achieved with relative success, but only at the expense of sluggish economic growth and widespread suffering among the working class and peasantry. That was hardly the most prudent policy option for an anaemic economy. Second, the Mission hoped that the banks would be discouraged from extending large credits to the private sector without adequate reserves, especially since a sizeable portion of the loans were directed toward speculative ventures. Third, the Law required the commercial banks to submit monthly statements of their business loans to the Currency Committee which was the overseer of Greece's financial network. Finally, the banking system became rigidly centralized under the Currency Committee's authority because Greece's finances were enhanced to a limited degree by the stimulation which American aid provided.[19]

The second paragraph of Article II of Law No. 588 vividly illustrates the regimentation of Greece's financial network under the Currency Committee. It stated that:

> The Currency Committee shall determine from time to time by its decisions the details of the financing of each branch of production, the total amounts of credits to be granted and the terms and preliminary conditions under which they are to be made available by banks, other credit organizations or any other kind of public law organization whatsoever, either out of their own funds or out of funds made available to them by the Bank of Greece.[20]

The Currency Committee enjoyed more comprehensive powers in Greece than any other public or private entity. The destiny of Greece's finances/economy, therefore, rested in the hands of American officials.

C. A. Munkman noted that between 1948 and 1952 'all expenditures of capital development, directly or indirectly, were controlled by the American Mission'. The American officials in Greece enjoyed such unprecedented authority over Greek financial affairs partly because of two key agreements that were signed in 1948. The National Mortgage Bank of Greece, the Government and the AMAG signed an agreement on 30 March 1948, which provided $3.9 million for the development of the mining and manufacturing sectors. The second agreement, which the government, the Mission and the Agricultural Bank of Greece signed on 5 May, provided $7 million to stimulate growth in agriculture and fisheries. Considering that American foreign assistance to Greece between fiscal 1947–1948 and 1950–1951 amounted to an incredible $1,672.6 billion, the funds allocated for mining, agriculture, manufacturing and fisheries were neglible. Furthermore, it was a small price to pay for the United States government whose mission regimented Greece's economy.[21]

The Currency Commission continued to regulate the operations of the banking system throughout the Civil War. In January 1949 the commercial banks were compelled to hold 22 percent of their resources in reserve for the demand and time deposits of public organizations and 10 percent for all other deposits. 'A year later reserve requirements increased once again; this time banks were required to hold in reserve 25 percent of the demand and time deposits of public agencies and corporations and 12 percent of all other demand and time deposits.' As the banking system became more centralized under the auspices of the Mission, the Bank of Greece assumed more authority in the country's financial structure.[22]

The American Mission enjoyed as much influence in Greece's fiscal policy as it did in monetary and credit policies. The AMAG initiated a programme of increased indirect taxes, a wage/salary freeze across the board, and credit controls in March 1948. Governor Griswold anticipated that such measures would reduce inflation, stabilize the currency and generate more revenues to cover the chronic budget deficits. The Mission authorized a 25 percent increase for cigarettes and an 8 percent increase for bread. Such policies were extremely burdensome to the lower classes and stifled development. Nevertheless, Ambassador Grady estimated that revenues generated from indirect taxes would reduce the prospective 1948–1949 budget deficit by 600 billion drachmas and the money saved would then be devoted to reconstruction projects.

Unfortunately, the precipitous rise in taxes which coincided with price increases proved inflationary and the budget deficits soared as the defence expenditures burgeoned amidst the Civil War. Consequently, the Mission's fiscal policy was unpopular for it failed in its purpose. Organized labour, whose leadership was sympathetic to the regime and the Mission, objected vehemently to the wage/salary freeze policy because prices were allowed to rise and income taxes as well as business taxes were not considered as alternative methods of raising revenues. Moreover, the actual budget deficit for 1948–1949 was grossly underestimated by the American officials in Athens, leaving the politicians seriously concerned. The national budget, which was prepared under the Mission's supervision, was submitted to Parliament on September 28, 1948; three months after the previous fiscal year had ended. The reason for the long delay was that Ambassador Grady actually vetoed the Administration's bloated budget in July as it did not conform to his directives.[23]

An Indian newspaper excoriated Grady's veto and questioned the stipulations which Washington placed on all foreign aid. The article explained Grady's overbearing role in Greek internal affairs as follows:

> Dr. Grady sends a strong note to the Greek Government vetoeing the Greek Budget on the ground that it contains expenditures other than agreed upon between the Greek Government and the American Mission . . . The important point is that, wise or foolish, good or bad, it is the Budget drawn up and agreed upon by the Greek Government and vetoed by an American Ambassador. And a country's budget is the expression of its policy in the exercise of its sovereignty. Where then does the sovereignty of Greece lie? Until this question is fully elucidated, there will be some uneasiness in debtor nations and the would-be-borrowers will become more cautious.[24]

The United States government justified its inordinate powers in Greece on the grounds that American aid kept the regime from collapse and the country from falling under communist control.

Appropriations for defence expenditures totalled 1,974 billion drachmas and non-military appropriations amounted to 1,949 billions. The projected deficit for fiscal 1948–1949 was 700 billion drachmas, but 500 billions would have been covered by foreign aid. Hence, the estimated deficit was 200 billion drachmas. The fiscal planners assumed that the Civil War would end in 1948 and had not calculated the extraordinary defence expenditures in the budget. Military and refief expenditures were estimated with a 25 percent reduction rate in the first half of the fiscal year to be followed by a 50 percent reduction in the second half. Since the guerrilla war ended in October 1949, the military and relief savings were not realized and supplementary expenditures for those sectors were required, thereby resulting in still higher deficits.[25]

The conservative and liberal press assailed the government in Washington for not providing sufficient assistance for

Greece and driving the country deeper into debt. One newspaper, *Kathimerini*, maintained that, according to the
Supreme Council of Reconstruction Committee's report,
the prospective budget deficit would be one trillion drachmas,
not 200 billion as the Mission estimated. Other newspapers
pointed out that ERP funds were unjustly transferred from
vital reconstruction programmes to the defence budget.

The ECA/G authorized the Greek government to divert
500 billion drachmas from the reconstruction programme to
cover the budget deficit for fiscal 1948-1949. The total
expenditures for the fiscal year amounted to 4,387 billion
drachmas, leaving a 937 billion drachmas deficit. To avert a
possible wrecking of the state's finances, American officials
hastily recommended raising direct taxes, while at the same
time they imposed drastic reductions on non-defence spending. The government adopted the above measures and reduced
the deficit to 622 billion drachmas which was covered by
the counterpart fund.[26]

Budget deficits persisted throughout the post-war years
partly because of the regressive tax structure and the ever-
rising defence spending. Military expenditures absorbed
47 percent of the budget, or 9.4 percent of the entire national
income between 1948 and 1952. The net indebtedness of the
state to the Bank of Greece continued to soar after the
Truman Doctrine. The following chart illustrates the trend of
government borrowing.

In Billion of Drachmas[27]

1947	1948	1949	1950	1951	1952
882	1,097	2,861	3,549	5,577	6,057

The defence budget grew progressively higher after the Civil
War ended, thus it cannot be argued that exigent conditions
merited such exorbitant spending.

The Organization for European Economic Co-operation,
OEEC, an agency responsible for European economic integration created after the enunciation of the Marshall Plan,
concluded in its 1952 report that the defence budget of
Greece absorbed a great percentage of the GNP. It stated that:

The increase in defence expenditure will absorb, between 1951 and
1953-54, about 22 percent of the increase in the gross national

product at factor cost; the percentage of the gross national product absorbed by the defence expenditure will rise from 8.6 in 1951 to 9.3 in 1953–54.[28]

To place this issue into a broader perspective, the following chart provides a lucid comparison of the defence allocations of six NATO countries in fiscal 1952–53.

Greece	42 percent of the Budget[29]			
Turkey	33	”	”	”
Italy	23	”	”	”
France	32	”	”	”
Holland	27	”	”	”
Belgium	23	”	”	”

The conservative governments in Athens, which the United States backed, opted for a strong defence, especially as relations between Greece and Turkey were strained over the Cyprus issue. Ultimately, however, responsibility for the disproportionate defence spending lies with Washington which provided Greece with military assistance and policy advice on strategic affairs.

The American Mission announced in 1952 that the United States government decided to discontinue subsidizing the Greek budget. The Government of Prime Minister Alexandros Papagos, which was installed by the Americans, retaliated immediately. As Munkman put it:

The impossibility of establishing budgetary equilibrium without cutting military expenditure is obvious. Consequently the Greek Government and press stated that unless the United States supported the budget by a definite grant, the army establishment would be cut. As a result a specific grant (described as for military aid) was provided to meet the 1953–54 deficit of 750 million drachmas increased to 1,050 million in 1954–55 estimates ($1 = 30 drachmas).[30]

The United States retained its pre-eminent influence in the Greek military establishment and exerted more control over the country's defence policy than the indigenous military High Command. This was made possible because of American military aid to Greece. Finally, it must be stressed that since 1947 Greek defences were designed to suit the United States global policy of containment, rather than Greece's regional requirements. There has been a consensus in Greece on this issue, regardless of political affiliations and ideological leanings. The first attempt to redirect the defences to meet the country's own requirements was made in 1981 by Prime Minister Andreas Papandreou.[31]

After the termination of the Civil War, General Van Fleet concluded that American strategic interests in Greece were not simply designed to eliminate the threat of communism, but to install a permanent presence in the country that would police the menacing Communist bloc. According to Van Fleet:

> The geo-political position and military strategic position of Greece remain unchanged from the time 'Truman' doctrine was announced. However, it appears that the strategic control of the mediterranean area by US has increased since that announcement. Greece offers an important base for the collection of strategic intelligence . . . US year to year policy must be changed to a long term policy. *The US is here to stay.* Greece can be secondary front to Soviet diversion in event of war. Also its strategic position has greatly increased. Greeks will fight, are a good investment.[32]

Eventually, Athens became one of the major centres of Central Intelligence Agency operations and Greece the host of American military bases. Greece, Turkey and Iran – the Northern Tier – became part of an American regional strategic network, subordinating their own national security interests to those of the United States.

E. The Four Year Plan in Greece

Ambassador Grady delivered a speech on 28 November 1948 on Athens radio regarding the relevance of the Marshall Plan to Greece. He emphasized that the ERP was above all a humanitarian programme and added that the United States was resolved to undertake the revitalization of the devastated European economy for the sake of peace, prosperity, and the containment of communism. He then introduced the Greek Four Year Plan which he underlined was purely a 'Greek plan, drawn by your Ministers and technicians after long and careful study of the many complex problems which the country faces today.' He admitted that the Greek officials 'worked closely with their American colleagues', but he did not point out that members of his Embassy and Mission were the chief architects of the plan.

Stefanos Stefanopoulos, Minister of Co-ordination, also delivered a speech on the virtues of the Marshall Plan and the Four Year Plan. He did not divulge the specifics of the programme because the OEEC had not approved it. He stressed, however, that: 'The economic problem of Greece is characterized by inadequacy of cultivatable land and shortage of capital equipment in the country on the one hand and by a rapid increase of the population on the other'. The Minister of Co-ordination maintained that unemployment and chronic underemployment must be eliminated if the nation would experience substantial economic recovery. The general objectives of the Reconstruction Plan were outlined as follows:

1. Execution of large projects for a speedy industrialization of the country. 2. Exploitation of hydraulic energy to secure cheap electric power and development of solid fuel (lignite) in the country to develop power in Greece are set as basic prerequisites for industrialization. The exploitation of hydraulic energy will also facilitate the progress of agriculture, a revival of the countryside and a checking of movement of rural dwellers toward the cities, in combination with execution of hydraulic and land improvement projects on a large scale.[33]

According to the Minister's estimates, 40 percent of the total investment under the plan was to be spent on industrial development.

Hydro-electricity was given priority as the foundation for rebuilding the infrastructure and eventually for industrializing the country. Industrialization, however, as defined by the plan entailed the exploitation of minerals. There were no plans to build new industries in locations other than the capital which was already overpopulated. The development of water power took precedence because it would reduce the nation's dependence on expensive imported fuels, while making possible the rise of agricultural output, flood control and drainage works. It is interesting to note that the United States entertained a general policy of fostering the development of the infrastructure and agricultural sectors of Third World economies. Projects similar to those of Greece, for example, were under way in many Latin American countries during the same period and were financed by North American credits and loans.

Stefanopoulos predicted that by 1950 industrial production would rise to 115 percent of the pre-war level and agricultural production to 119 percent of the pre-war level. He expected a 10 percent reduction in imports of consumer goods and a 70 percent increase in imports of construction materials. Exports were expected to rise 26 percent above pre-war levels and an additional 280,000 jobs would be created by the Four Year Plan. Finally, the Minister accurately predicted that the balance of payments deficit would not be eradicated by the programme because Greece was not expected to reduce its debt and foreign trade deficit.[34]

The Four Year Plan was doomed to fail from its inception for several reasons. First, it required immense United States economic aid on a long term basis 'whereas it was the practice of Congress to vote appropriations to ECA for one year ahead only'. Second, it was inadequately funded because the governments in Washington and Athens reduced reconstruction expenditures at various intervals during the programme. Third, there was gross abuse of funds by Greek administrators. Fourth, the Plan emphasized the development of infrastructure and the primary sector of production with no mention of the capital goods sector. Finally, authority for funds appropriation for all projects rested with the Mission, not the Greek government. Consequently, American officials made decisions to finance projects they deemed necessary for the country, rather than allowing the local authorities to make such decisions.

The question regarding the plan's financing is most perplexing because funds that were originally earmarked for economic aid were transferred to defence and economic aid funds which were earmarked for industrial projects went for agriculture or other sectors. The internal cost of the programme was estimated at $600 million on the basis of the Greek 1948 price level at 6 trillion drachmas. The Mission estimated the cost of the plan at $546 million, of which $343 million emanated from American aid and $203 million from Greece's own resources. For fiscal 1948–1949 the ECA/G approved $67.4 million for reconstruction and development and for the uncovered dollar deficit. Of the above sum, $3.1 million was in dollar aid, $46.3 million was in ERP drawing rights and $18 million was to be contributed from the Greek sterling resources which constituted part of the British war debt. Of the total annual aid package amounting to $390.6 million for fiscal 1948–1949, only $49.4 million was allocated for reconstruction and development and a substantial part of that was cover for the country's dollar deficit.[35]

Greece financed part of the Four Year Plan from the $105 million reparations settlement with Italy. According to the Greek–Italian Agreement, which was signed on 31 August 1949, the reparations were discharged in five annual instalments in the form of industrial machinery and tools, several ships, and consumer goods. Greece also received an additional $10 million in reparations from Germany and it too was devoted to the reconstruction programme. Its own resources, however, were still insufficient to finance the Four Year Plan.

The ECA in Paris did not fully endorse the Greek Plan and the ERP administrator, Paul Hoffman, an American businessman, did not believe that the programme would be completed on schedule. In the spring of 1950 the original plan was revised because very little had been accomplished hitherto. In the revised programme communications and electrical power were earmarked for 23.5 percent and 14.3 percent respectively of the total programme expenditure. Agriculture and fisheries were to receive 13.2 percent, while industry was earmarked for 17.9 percent. The remainder of the designated $663.5 million reconstruction package was for housing, public health, land reclamation, mining, sanitation and water supply projects, education, refugee rehabilitation and tourism. The Four Year Plan had proved unsuitable for the country's needs and, as will be seen below, even the plan that was finally implemented ended in failure.[36]

F. The Failure of ERP in Greece

The basic infrastructure of Greece was largely completed by the end of the Four Year Plan, but industrialization was not achieved for it was not one of the objectives of the American planners. The object of the reconstruction programme was to foster the primary sector of production and retain Greece as an exporter of raw materials and an importer of manufactured goods and capital. Furthermore, the reconstruction plan was designed to pave the way for direct foreign investment. 'Under the initial AMAG programme,' wrote Munkman, 'continued under the ECA, groups of American contractors moved into Greece to rebuild the Port of Piraeus, open the Corinth Canal, repair the damaged railways, and build or repair principal strategic roads.'[37]

Some construction projects were defective because of rampant corruption and lack of proper supervision. Ambassador Grady noted in June 1949 that the civil authorities in Patras were accused of misusing ECA funds that were appropriated for work relief projects. A State Department report revealed in September 1949 that 'the Greek highways rebuilt under American construction program were breaking up already due to poor engineering or materials, hasty construction during winter weather for military reasons, etc.' There were considerable repairs on faulty road construction which contributed to the overall cost-overrun of the reconstruction projects. Commenting on the abuses of the reconstruction programme by contractors and public officials, Professor Stavrianos wrote:

> Roger D. Lapham, the ECA chief in Greece, disclosed on April 19, 1951, that two American highway construction advisers were asked to leave Greece. A dozen Greek contractors and members of the Ministry of Public Order were being investigated concerning irregularities involving $500,000, and the Greek Government was asked to rebate $100,000 mispent on one road project.[38]

It is interesting to note that American firms had a reputation of defective and costly work and of dealing with corrupt public officials in many underdeveloped countries. There was a big scandal in Ecuador, for example, involving an American construction firm charged with the task of building the Quevedo–Manta Highway during the mid-1940s. There too, American funds and advisers were used to help build the country's infrastructure. There was indeed a pattern of abuses involving American aid or loans to the Third World, American businesses and local public officials.

The American officials in Athens were in the paramount position to help launch the country into the age of industrialization so that it would be able to compete effectively with the other European countries. Instead the Mission chose to retain Greece in the periphery sector of the world-economy. This was accomplished by the manipulation of the credit network as well as the fiscal and monetary policies for which the American advisers were responsible. The Central Loan Committee, which was dominated by American officials and which enjoyed veto power over every loan, initially financed eight loans totalling $9,133,700. By July 1949 the Committee had approved twenty-five loans amounting to $17,540,524. The British-owned Athens–Piraeus Electricity Company was the recipient of the largest loan, while companies manufacturing chemicals, cement, copper, paper, and other essential materials were also granted loans.[39]

Long term loans for the revitalization of private businesses amounted to $12,987,000 in 1949 to be spent abroad and 33,343 million drachmas to be spent domestically. The amounts increased to $40,343,000 and 260,000 million drachmas respectively in 1950. The above funds emanated from foreign aid and the Counterpart Account. The Central Loan Committee guaranteed $80.5 million during its existence between 1948 and 1954. All loans were repayable in dollars and were allocated as follows: '52.4 percent to manufacturing, 14.7 percent to agriculture and fishing, 13.4 percent to mining, 12.4 to power, 5.4 percent to communications and transportation and 1.7 percent to tourism.' The aggregate bank credits to the economy from 1949 to 1952 were 18,988 billion drachmas, of which 3,125 billions were devoted to industry. The value of industrial production showed a significant recovery under the Marshall Plan, but that cannot be attributed to the ECA's plans to industrialize Greece since only light industry experienced growth. Thus, there was vertical expansion — established industries benefited — rather than horizontal development — new industries — in the secondary sector of the economy. In any event, industrial production was 87 percent of the 1939 level in 1949, while in 1951 it reached a peak at 125 in comparison to the pre-war level. Thereafter, industry experienced a period of stagnation because economic aid was severely limited and the banks were compelled to curtail credit allocation to fight inflation.[40]

Neither the indigenous capitalist class nor the government made any genuine efforts in the late 1940s and early 1950s to industrialize Greece to comparable levels of most East European countries. The American Mission, therefore, was not solely responsible for the lack of Greek industrial development. The private and public sectors invested the lowest percentage of the national income in comparison to other European nations as the chart below indicates.

Area[41]	National Income Invested in Production
Greece	8.5 percent
West Germany	23 "
Scandinavia	30 "
Western Europe	15-30 "

The above statistics are applicable for 1952, but Greek investment in productive works remained the lowest in Europe throughout the 1950s and never exceeded 10 percent of the national income. The following chart delineates the percentage of public investment in the various sectors of the economy between 1948 and 1952.

Transportation[42]	36.9
Housing	17.0
Electrical Power	8.6
Agriculture, Forestry, Fisheries	16.8
Mining & Manufacturing	1.7
Public Administration	18.8

The state devoted most of its investment capital to the infrastructure and the primary sector of production at the expense of investment in heavy industry. That policy was in accord with the American advice since 1947, but the Greek state and capitalist class were resigned to the fact that structural development would be unrealistic for a country with limited capital resources, technicians and scientists.

Andreas Papandreou, who served as Director of the Centre for Economic Research in the early 1960s, wrote in 1962 that the Four Year Plan (the 1950 version) had not achieved its own objectives of 'development of resources, a reduction of unemployment and the achievement of a tolerable standard of living'. He argued that Greece's monumental economic problems could have been rectified only by the development of the secondary sector of production.[43]

Industrialization was possible under the ECA programme, but it was deliberately precluded for a number of reasons. Greece received $648 million under the AMAG programme but only $119 million was actually allocated for economic assistance. Under the ECA plan the government received $550 million in economic aid, but only $150 million was spent on reconstruction and economic development. The remaining $400 million was used to cover the budget deficits and the balance of payments deficits. Defence spending and the financing of American imports, therefore, absorbed the capital resources which could have been devoted for economic development.

The Counterpart Account funds were sufficient to enhance the financing of the Four Year Plan, but the Mission blocked them. In 1948 there were 219,801 million unused drachmas in that Account, while in 1952 the amount soared to 7,446,362 millions. Those funds were ostensibly intended for agricultural and industrial development, but the United States officials in Athens did not release the funds for a number of reasons. First, the circulation of such an immense amount of money would have created even higher monetary inflation in the volatile economy at a time when the Mission's primary goal was to bring down inflation. Second, the funds were held back to cover the budget and balance of payments deficits. Third, the Counterpart Account, as Munkman noted, was the key to the Mission's control of Greece's monetary policy. Finally, United States foreign economic policy was not designed to foster the industrial development of underdeveloped countries, but to perpetuate the export-oriented segment of those economies.[44]

Before elucidating fully the precise method which the Mission adopted to prevent Greece from industrializing, it should be pointed out that the country's commercial dependence on the United States was one of the factors in the former's inability to industrialize. The government in Athens and the ECA/G deliberated on the balance of payments issue in June 1949. They proposed the following measures: 'a. flexible subsidies to be obtained through corresponding import levies, b. multiple exchange rates for imports and exports, and c. general revaluation of the drachma to a more realistic rate.' Greece imported at the rate of $450 million annually and exported at the rate of $150 million in 1949. The above measures were designed to redress the gross trade imbalance which American and Greek officials attributed to overpricing of Greek products in the world market, the inflated drachma and the loss of pre-war markets, especially Germany and Eastern Europe. The State Department and the International Monetary Fund, IMF, gave similar advice to other Third World nations which were dependencies of the West. Devaluation of the currency, curtailment of government spending on development projects and social programmes, liberalization of trade, restriction of credit extension and extension of lucrative terms to foreign investors has been the prescription which the IMF and the United States government passed on to underdeveloped countries since Bretton Woods in 1944. The results have been greater dependence on the United States by the periphery countries and inability to foster independent industrial development.[45]

The responsibility for the balance of payments deficit rested particularly with the Foreign Trade Administration, FTA, which was headed by an American official. The FTA's policies were designed to stimulate the export sector and perpetuate the consumerist-oriented economy of Greece. The balance of payments deficit before the war was 16 percent of the total foreign payments and the country's exports covered 60 percent of the imports. In 1952 under *American-okratia* the exports covered only 28 percent of the imports and the balance of payments deficit was 55 to 60 percent of the aggregate foreign payments. The OEEC report of 1952 stated that: 'The deficit in the balance of payments on current account which was about 60 percent of external expenditure from 1948 to 1952 and will remain very high in the coming years, is certainly the most urgent problem for the Greek economy.'[46]

The United States government assistance programme subsidized a large percentage of Greece's balance of payments deficit for the duration of the ERP. It was precisely that process which led to foreign trade and financial dependence of the United States once aid ended and was replaced by trade. Table A below compares the per capita trade of Greece with other OEEC members in 1951 and it shows that the former remained a net importer, while the latter recovered much faster under the Marshall Plan. Table B compares Greece's imports covered by exports against other ERP recipients and shows the degree to which the former lagged behind other countries.

79

TABLE A[47]

Country	Imports	Exports
Greece	$52.39	$13.38
France	106.92	98.25
Germany	69.40	68.80
Italy	45.33	34.86
Turkey	19.20	15.00

TABLE B

Greece	28%
Turkey	78%
Italy	77%
France	92%

It is important to emphasize that 90 percent of Greece's foreign trade during the early Cold War was with North America and Western Europe. Trade diversification, which was absolutely imperative for the country's economic as well as political interests, was precluded by trade dependence on the West. The government in Washington prevented Greece from engaging in regional economic integration by discouraging commercial relations with Eastern Europe, the Soviet Union and to a lesser extent the Arab World. Given Greece's geographical proximity to the aforementioned countries, it was contrary to its interests not to have extensive relations with them.[48]

The American Mission had publicly vowed to make Greece self-sufficient through the aid programme. Although self-sufficiency should not be misconstrued as autarchy since that is impossible in a world of inter-dependence, the general idea was that Greece would attain a balance in its foreign payments. The ECA country report of 1949 concluded that Greece could not achieve peace, financial stability, reconstruction and development without foreign aid. Upon the termination of the ERP, the nation was less self-sufficient and had not achieved the reconstruction and development goals which the ECA/G set for itself. One critic of American intervention in Greece wrote the following concerning the results of foreign aid.

For all the grandiose talk about reconstruction there has been no reconstruction in Greece. Both industrial and agricultural levels of the country are still (in the middle of 1950) below pre-war levels. General William A. Methany, former chief of the Air Section of the

U.S. Military Mission in Greece, told a *Christian Science Monitor* reporter (on September 8, 1949) that only 15 percent of the many millions of dollars we have poured into Greece during the past two-and-a-half years have gone to help the economic recovery of the country. All the rest has gone for direct and indirect army expenditures.[49]

Military expenditures, as stated above, took precedence over economic development programmes. Based on the Greek government's records, American economic aid to Greece for fiscal 1947–1948 and fiscal 1949–1950 was earmarked at $760.7 million and military at $476.8 million.

Of the cumulative aid amounting to $1,237.5 million for the three-year period under AMAG and ECA, only $232 million was actually spent on reconstruction and economic development. Indubitably, aid did stimulate economic growth, but it did not contribute to Greece's structural development. One economist drew the following conclusion concerning appropriation of aid funds to Greece.

> During these two years (fiscal 1948–1949 and 1949–1950) economic aid (earmarked at $530.5 million) was used either directly or indirectly for military expenditures and also for purposes of keeping the economy going on a day-to-day basis. So while other countries were using aid to reconstruct their economies and build a solid basis for later growth, Greece had to spend her share on purposes far removed from economic development.[50]

Unlike other members of the Organization for European Economic Co-operation, OEEC, Greece was immersed in a costly Civil War. Damages to property resultant from the guerrilla war have been estimated at $250 million and military expenditures at $750 million. Based on an unofficial source, the Civil War absorbed 84.7 percent of the cumulative foreign aid which Greece received to the end of 1949. The total foreign aid amounted to $2,138 million, of which $1,812 million accounted for losses sustained due to the guerrilla war. The bulk of American aid, therefore, was devoted to the military and not economic development.[51]

Despite the enormous cost of the Civil War, it was possible for Greece to initiate industrial development under the ECA/G. The American Mission, however, as noted above, did not have such plans. The ECA and the State Department had decided that Greece did not have an industrial base or the technical personnel to industrialize as was the case for

Western Europe. It was decided, therefore, that Greece must develop its mining, agriculture, fisheries and consumer goods industries; in short the established sectors. Paul Hoffman reflected this view in a 1949 ECA report. In proposing the most efficacious method to alleviate underemployment in the countryside, he stated that:

> New and expanded food and other processing, manufacturing and mining industry can provide the basis for this employment. Essentially Greece needs to look to the development of industries requiring relatively large amount employment per $1000 of product and not the development of heavy industries requiring large investments per worker.[52]

The above formula was a prescription for perpetual underdevelopment and a number of contemporary Greek officials and scholars disagreed with Hoffman's and the State Department's view regarding Greece's industrialization.

The Secretary General of the Supreme Reconstruction Council, S. Agapitidis, argued in an article published in 1950 that industrialization was the only possible solution for reducing Greece's unemployment and structural underemployment. He maintained that 60 percent of the rural population was far in excess of the required labour force to cultivate the land. Even with the modest modernization of agriculture, which promised to make more land available for cultivation, there was still 20 percent surplus labour in the countryside. 'Only industrialization,' wrote Agapitides, 'could absorb the country's surplus manpower.'[53]

Studies conducted under the auspices of the Centre for Economic Research in Athens during the early 1960s, arrived at the same conclusion as Agapitidis. Professor Angelopoulos estimated that in 1953 one million of the four million people in the labour force were idle as unemployment and underemployment among peasants stood at 40 percent. The OEEC Report of 1952 corroborated the figures and conclusions that Angelopoulos reached. Urban unemployment according to OEEC was about 150,000, while rural unemployment and underemployment was one million. Yet there was nothing, except promises, in the Four Year Plan to redress this catastrophic problem which plagued Greece throughout the 1950s.[54]

The country's valuable mineral deposits, especially bauxite which was in abundance, were part of the answer to the question of industrialization. Hugh Seton-Watson noted in his illuminating study on Eastern Europe that:

> Greece more than any East European country needs a programme of planned industrialization. Its foundations can only be the mineral resources and water power of the country. Instead of exporting minerals, Greece must work them in her own industry and export the more valuable semi-finished products.[55]

Land, mines, and labour were all under-utilized partly because the American advisers discouraged central planning along the lines followed by the Communist countries or even a policy mix of state and private initiated industrial development.

Despite the progress which most Eastern European nations made by undertaking the structural development of their economies by central planning, Greece failed to emulate her neighbours due to political as well as socioeconomic considerations. The American Mission was the major obstacle in that regard. It rejected the Greek government's proposal to exploit the coal deposits of Central Macedonia. The bauxite mines fell under the semi-control of the Americans since it is well-known that bauxite is one strategic mineral that the United States lacks. The rich mineral resources were not utilized as the basis for industrial development because that would have entailed statist policies, which the American advisers vehemently opposed. It would have meant also sweeping agrarian reforms and agricultural modernization to create a mobile labour force, combined with drastic changes in the consumerist-oriented economy. Such dramatic changes were simply impossible given the existing power structure and its ties to the United States.

The German government offered Greece a steel mill as part of reparations payment in 1949. Paul Porter used his veto privilege to prevent Greece from engaging in steel production. Consequently, the country was compelled to purchase steel as well as other metals from the developed countries. That case exemplified the manner by which the American officials in Athens obstructed the progress of Greece. As already stated, however, the State Department entertained the same policies toward Third World nations in general. When the government in Colombia endeavoured to build a steel mill in 1948, an IBRD Mission to that country advised against it and rejected funding for the project. The Mission maintained that it was cheaper for Colombia to purchase steel from the United States than to produce it locally. In many cases, therefore, foreign aid and loans were not designed to help the development of the Third World, but prevent it.[56]

The Greek representative at the OEEC was convinced that the United States and Western Europe precluded Greece from industrializing in the late 1940s and early 1950s.

> Industrialization met with certain reaction mainly because of its effects on the foreign trade of the interested countries, but also largely because of the economic self sufficiency of Greece, which would have resulted from it, in a few years' time. Thus it was commercial, economic and political interests that imposed on the countries that part (in the American missions) an unqualified hostility towards all plans for industrialization.[57]

The bulk of American exports to Greece consisted of surplus agricultural products, but there were also exports of dubious use to the mass consumer. Finally, it should be noted that after 1953, when economic aid was gradually phased out in favour of trade, American exports to Greece consisted of consumer goods which the host government did not deem indispensable to the economy.

The more serious short term failures of the ECA/G were in connection with the refugee population and the taxation issue. The American Mission had assumed the responsibility of assisting with the refugee problem, but was unable to accomplish a great deal. Ambassador Grady informed the State Department in June 1949 that there were 600,000 people in security camps who were in dire need of housing, jobs, farm equipment and other means to enable them to start over again after the guerrilla war. Many farmers returned to their homes only to discover that their property was destroyed. Others went to the cities seeking employment at a time when there were very few jobs for unskilled labour.[58]

After the Civil War the refugee population was gradually reduced, but its remnants lingered on throughout the early 1950s. Constantine Karamanlis, Minister for Co-ordination and future Prime Minister, disclosed the following information in September 1949 concerning the condition of the refugees.

> The misery of the countryside is immense. Moreover, of the evacuated peasants, 1,033,000 are paupers receiving assistance. Eight hundred and eighteen thousand are receiving financial assistance from the

state. Thirty four thousand orphans are dependent on the state. A hundred and fifty-eight thousand peasant families are far from their homes and many of them have lost all their property.[59]

Despite the government's efforts to mitigate the refugee tragedy, there were still 450,000 people in that predicament in summer 1950 and the effects of the refugee phenomenon were felt for many years thereafter.

The effects of Anglo-American intervention are lucidly discernible in the standard of living indices during the early Cold War. From 1945 to 1953, the years when Greece received billions of dollars in foreign assistance and was subjected to foreign intervention, the cost of living index jumped from 1,895 to 4ト,280, while the notes in circulation increased from 104 billion drachmas to 2,971 billions. It was during that period that Anglo-American advisers exerted enormous influence in Greek internal affairs. British and American advisers were in the propitious position to introduce a sound tax structure for Greece, especially considering the incessant criticism from London and Washington on this issue. Yet there was no fundamental tax reform and the low income families continued to bear the burden of taxation.[60]

Direct taxes in fiscal 1948–1949, according to the Greek government, accounted for 17.3 percent of all revenues, while in fiscal 1951–1952 direct taxation was equal to − in constant drachmas − the 1938–1939 level. Total revenues for fiscal 1951–1952 were at par with fiscal 1938–1939. Wray O. Candilis has written that:

> But as incomes in 1951 were higher than prewar ones, taxation became consequently lighter. Incomes of businessmen and corporations were at least double in 1951 compared to 1938, while taxes were approximately the same; this meant that their burden was half of what it was. Furthermore, tax evasion was widespread, especially among high income groups, and no measures were taken to establish a tax system that could be both effective and simple and would provide the necessary incentives for investment and economic development.[61]

There were tax reforms under the Mission's initiative, but they affected indirect taxes which were regressive. Few adjustments were made in income taxes and the lower classes continued to bear the brunt of taxation under an archaic tax structure. Although the Greek regime must assume responsibility ultimately for failing to rectify this problem, the American advisers behind the regime played a significant role in the government's fiscal affairs.

The numerous shortcomings of the ECA/G had a far reaching impact on contemporary Greece. The American Mission was concerned principally with the geopolitical importance of Greece and reduced the country to a military satellite and an economic dependency of the advanced capitalist countries. The military establishment, the bureaucracy, the conservative and centrist politicians, and the capitalist class were responsible for collaborating with the United States government in a desperate attempt to prevent a possible change in the patronage system, the power structure and the *status quo* in general. Consequently, Greece failed to make economic progress comparable to that of either its Eastern or Western European neighbours during the Cold War and it failed to solve the issue of social justice which was one of the primary reasons for social revolution in the 1940s.

G. From Foreign Aid to Private Investment

American government aid, Export–Import Bank and IBRD credits as well as other forms of economic assistance have been used invariably by Republican and Democratic administrations in Washington since President Roosevelt to stimulate the expansion of American businesses. Greece had a limited potential as a market and as a supplier of raw materials in comparison to larger Third World countries such as Brazil, Chile, Iran, etc. However, the United States Mission laid the foundations for the eventuality of massive foreign capital penetration in Greece.

The transition from aid to trade and foreign capital investment took place in the early 1950s as American aid was almost exclusively military after Greece was inducted into NATO. United States officials informed the government in Athens in February 1951 that Greece must restrict commercial credit, restrict the distribution of basic foodstuffs, which were either given away or sold at reduced prices, and revise the Recovery Program to allow for the enhancement of military projects. All of the above measures were recommended to prepare the government to cope with reduced foreign assistance. The Greeks complied with the austere policy recommendations which resulted in sluggish economic growth during the early 1950s.

The United States Government cancelled all aid for the Greek reconstruction programme in 1951 unless the projects had already started. Economic aid was reduced from $181 million in fiscal 1951–1952 to $21.3 million in fiscal 1953–1954. Paul Porter explained that the drastic cuts in economic assistance were designed as 'punishment' for the Greek government which refused to seek out tax evaders and curtail budgetary spending. There can be no doubt that the Greeks were guilty of those charges, but there is no correlation between the foreign aid reductions and the remiss conduct of the pro-American regime in Athens. Once the Greek Communist Party was thoroughly crushed and the country was firmly in the Western sphere of influence, there was no need for the United States to continue economic assistance to Greece. Foreign aid undermined private trade and was not in accord with the principles of the Bretton Woods system.[62]

American businesses started investing in Greece gradually after the end of the Civil War and escalated such activity after 1953. Paul Porter assured a group of American investors on 10 November 1949 that Greece was a lucrative area for investment because wages were low and were not likely to rise. American firms gained control after 1949 of major construction and water works projects and invested in mining and industry. The government signed an exclusive contract in June 1949 with the International Telephone and Telegraph Company, an American-based transnational corporation, granting the company a monopoly of the country's communications network. The Greek News Agency in London reported on 4 August 1950 that:

> American-owned firms are replacing Greek firms, while American capital is securing a controlling position in many companies, nominally Greek. The International Telegraph Company announced on June 21, 1949 that it had assumed control of all communications in Greece through an autonomous company free from all governmental or ministerial control.[63]

The Greek government, acting on the advice of the American Mission, extended lucrative incentives to foreign investors. Prime Minister Alexander Papagos devalued the drachma on

April 9 1953 from 15,000 drachmas to 30,000 to the dollar. At the same time, he abolished special import taxes and export subsidies. Those measures were adopted at the insistence of the American government which gave similar advice to other Third World countries during the post-war years. The Minister of Co-ordination, Spyros Markezinis, admitted publicly on 4 September 1953 that the Papagos administration was impelled to implement the above measures because of pressure from the American Mission.[64]

A State Department memorandum, dated 4 August 1949, revealed that a staff of seven American policy makers planned 'the future path of [Greek] economic development and capital investment in Greece without the advice or consent of the Greek authorities'. The policy makers discussed plans for reducing aid to Greece for it had a negative impact on the standard of living. Large scale emigration and foreign direct investment were recommended as options to counterbalance the negative impact of cutting economic aid. Finally, the policy memo candidly stated that: 'Greece will achieve economic viability at some level, and that *we do have to decide what that level will be*.' The country's fate rested to a large degree with policy makers in Washington because they found various elements in Greece which were eager to collaborate.[65]

The transition from aid to foreign private investment was completed in October 1953 when the government in Athens enacted Law No. 2687 which dealt with the creation of advantageous conditions for foreign capital penetration. The Law was based on the following principles:

> 1. Guarantees against any kind of compulsory acquisition or government interference with foreign ownership enjoying the protection of the law; 2. The unchangeability of terms and conditions agreed upon; 3. The fixing of terms for repatriation of capital, profits and interest in foreign exchange; and 4. Creation of an especially advantageous system of taxation in favor of protected foreign capital.[66]

Under the new law, foreign investors were permitted to export profits up to 12 percent of the amount of imported capital. They had the option of receiving foreign exchange from Greek lending institutions and of discharging the service on their loans contracted abroad 'and for payment of interest up to 10 percent annually'. As foreign capital pervaded the Greek economy and took over key sectors during the 1950s, indigenous capital fled to the metropolis seeking higher profits and more secure investments. Capital flight was a general characteristic of Third World countries and it has been one of the key factors in the process of underdevelopment.[67]

The incentives and guarantees which the Greek government extended to foreign capital investors in 1953 were quite similar to those which authoritarian regimes in Colombia, Cuba, Peru, Taiwan, South Korea, and other countries in the periphery sector of the world-economy extended during the Cold War when the United States was at the zenith of its power. Greece had a great deal in common with other Third World countries which were military, political and economic dependencies of the United States. The unique characteristic of Greece was that it was an integral part of the NATO zone and its strategic location in the eastern mediterranean made it invaluable to the United States.

NOTES

1. For more details concerning the reception of the Truman Doctrine in Greek political circles see Smothers, Frank *et al. Report on the Greeks*, New York, 1948, 197–8; Rousseas, Stephen. *The Death of a Democracy*, New York, 1967, 87–8; Psyroukis, Nikos. *Istoria Synchronis Elladas* (History of Contemporary Greece), 3v., Athens, 1976, 1:195–6; *Public Papers of the Presidents. Harry S. Truman*, 1947, Washington, 1963, 180. For the Porter Mission recommendations see F.O. 371 GR 2609, No. OF 48/10/6; F.O. R1841, No. 342; FRUS 1947, 5:131–4; Theodoropoulos, Spyros. *Ap' to Dogma Truman sto Dogma Junta* (From the Truman Dogma to the Junta Dogma), Athens, 1976, 63–4; Economic Cooperation Administration, Greece Country Report, Washington, 1949, 2–3; Hugh Seton-Watson. *The East European Revolution*, 1950, 332; FRUS, 147, 5:136–7; Barnet, Richard J. *Intervention and Revolution*, New York, 1968, 123.
2. FRUS, 1947, 5:186.
3. William H. McNeill, *Greece: American Aid in Action, 1947–1956* (New York: The Twentieth Century Fund, 1957), 35.
4. FRUS. 1947, 5:177–8; Stavrianos, L. S. *Greece: American Dilemma and Opportunity*, Chicago, 1952, 193.
5. Sheppard, A. W. *Britain in Greece, London: League for Democracy in Greece*, 1947, 9; Agapitidis, S. 'Wage policy in Greece' in *International Labour Review*, 61 (1950), 243–4; FRUS, 1947, 5:204–5. For more details about the expenses of the Royal House see SDNA, 868.51/7–848, Office Memo. For more on the elaborate American propaganda machine see Department of State, *Second Report to Congress on the United States Relief Program*, Washington, 1947, 21. *Ib., Third Report to Congress on the United States Relief Program*, Washington, 1948, 37.
6. FO 371 R 340/14/19; FRUS, 1947, 5:76–7.
7. C. A. Munkman, *American Aid to Greece* (New York: Frederick A. Praeger, 1958), 63–4.

8. FRUS, 1947, 5:191-2.
9. FRUS, 1947, 5:291; Eudes, Dominique. *The Kapitanios*, English ed. London, 1972, 299; Candilis, Wray O. *The Economy of Greece 1946-1966*, New York, 1968, 71; Sweet-Escott, Bickham. *Greece: A Political and Economic Survey*, London, 1954, 192; SDNA, 868.516/5-747, No. 3,990; Smothers, op. cit., 72-4.
10. Foreign Commerce Yearbook, 1949, 91-2; FRUS, 1947, 5:341-2, 420-1; Candilis, op. cit., 49; FRUS, 1947, 5:413-4. For extensive details concerning Griswold's role in the Greek political arena, see G. Papandreou, *Politika Keimena* (Political Texts), Athens, 274-7; Katsoulis, Georgis D. *Istoria. tou Kommounistikou Kommatos Elladas* (History of the Greek Communist Party), 6v. Athens, 1980, 6:181; Rousseas, op. cit., 90; Stavrianos, op. cit., 187-9; Eudes, op. cit., 301; Woodhouse, C. M. *Apple of Discord*, London, 1948, 279.
11. SDNA, 868.5151/1-1648, No. 4.
12. *Second Report to Congress*, 18.
13. SDNA, 868.50/4-2348, No. 481, Enclosures 2-6; SDNA, 868.18/12-1947; Eudes, op. cit., 299.
14. SDNA, 868.00/12-1147; SDNA, 868.5017/11-147, No. 180.
15. Cited in SDNA, 868.5151/10-3147.
16. SDNA, 868.5017/11-147, No. 180; FRUS, 1947, 5:421; SDNA, 868/50/12-1147. Also *New York Times*, 12 October 1947. Professor Kariotis' research, which was based on archival material, confirmed the *New York Times* report that Griswold's powers were extensive and superceded the Greek Government's authority, Kariotis, Theodore C. 'American Economic Penetration of Greece in the Late Nineteen Forties' in *Journal of the Hellenic Diaspora*, 6 (Winter 1979), 91; FRUS, 1947, 5:378-88.
17. Ibid., 5:398.
18. McNeill, op. cit., 47; Katsoulis, op. cit., 6:237-9; *Foreign Commerce Yearbook*, 1951, 395, 380, 413, 517; Sweet-Escott, op. cit., 194.
19. SDNA 868.516/11-1848, No. 1, 121; A. A. Fatouros, 'Building Formal Structure of Penetration: The US in Greece, 1947-48' in Iatrides, J. (ed.) *Greece in the 1940s: A Nation in Crisis*, University Press of New England, 1981, 251; Candilis, op. cit., 46.
20. SDNA, 868.516/11-1848, No. 1,121.
21. Munkman, op. cit., 72; McNeill, op. cit., 229; Candilis, op. cit., 46.
22. Mouzelis, N. *Modern Greece: Facets of Underdevelopment*, London, 1978, 119; Candilis, op. cit., 48.
23. SDNA, 868.51/8-3048, AMAG-1,521; SDNA, 868.51/8-648, No. 239.
24. Cited in ibid., 868.51/8-648, No. 239.
25. SDNA, 868.51/10-848, No. 1,015.
26. SDNA, 868.50/5-148, No. 69; SDNA, 868.51/12-1249, No. 864. Direct taxes in fiscal 1948-1949 accounted for 17.3 percent of the revenues, or 501 billion drachmas. Indirect taxes were 82.7 percent of the revenues, or 2,391 billion drachmas. See SDNA, 868.5042/12-149, No. 6,991.
27. OEEC, *Progress and Problems of the European Economy* (Fifth Annual Report of the OEEC) (Paris, 1954), 124; Sweet-Escott, op. cit., 192; Munkman, op. cit., 71-2.
28. OEEC, *Europe the Way Ahead* (Fourth Annual Report to the OEEC) (Paris, 1952), 274.
29. Angelopoulos, Angelos. *Oikonomika Arthra kai Meletai 1946-1967* (Economic Articles and Studies 1946-1967), 2v. Athens, 1974, 1:301.
30. Munkman, op. cit., 71-2.
31. Ibid., 72. Nicholas A. Michas, 'Economic Development, Social Mobilization and the Growth of Public Expenditures in Greece', *American Journal of*

Economics and Sociology, 39 (1980): 39. Yiannis Roubatis, 'The United States and the Occupational Responsibilities of the Greek Armed Forces, 1947-1987', *Journal of the Hellenic Diaspora* 6 (1979): 39-57. For Papandreou's defense and foreign policy objectives see *Greek Government Programme Presented by the Prime Minister Andreas G. Papandreou* (Athens, 1981), 8-16.

32. FRUS, 1949, 6:454-5.
33. SDNA, 868.50/11-2748, No. 1,148. For more about Stefanopoulos see Meynaud, Jean *et al. Politikes Dynameis stin Ellada* (Political Forces in Greece), Athens, 1974, 89. For the entire text of the speech see SDNA, 868.50/11-2748, No. 1,148.
34. For the specifics of the Four Year Plan see ERP, *Greece*, 29, 30-4; SDNA, 868.50/11-2748, No. 1,148. FO 371 R 35/1102/19, No. 378; FO 371 R 11166/1102/19, No. 224; FO 371 R 8032/1102/19, No. 143E.
35. Sweet-Escott, op. cit., 108; ERP, *Greece*, 29-30, 42-3; FO 371 R 8032/1102/19, No. 143E; FRUS, 1949, 6:229.
36. SDNA, 868.50/9-2349, a-615. For more details about Hoffman and his functions see Hadley Arkes, *Bureaucracy and the Marshall Plan* (Princeton, NJ, Princeton University Press, 1972), 100-2. For more about the reconstruction programme see ERP, *Greece*, 111-2; also see FO 371 RG 1102/2, No. 78E.
37. Munkman, op. cit., 57; SDNA, 868.50/6-2749, A-406; SDNA, 868.50/9-1649, Office Memo.
38. Stavrianos, op. cit., 214-5.
39. SDNA, 868.50/7-2649, A-471.
40. FO 371 WG 1101/3, No. 32E; FO 371 RG 1102/18, No. 195E; FO 371 RG 1102/15, No. 190E; FO 371 RG 1101/1, No. 5; Candilis, op. cit., 57, 65; Psilos, Diomedes D. 'Postwar Economic Problems in Greece' in *Economic Development Issues: Greece, Israel, Taiwan and Thailand*. Committee for Economic Development, New York, 1968, 38; Sweet-Escott, op. cit.. 194.
41. Angelopoulos, op. cit., 1:297.
42. Candilis, op. cit., 146. The OEEC report of 1954 provided the following observation about the decline of investment in Greece's productive sector. '. . . gross investment measured at 1951 prices fell by 1,700 billion (27 percent) from 1951 to 1952, being no more than 12.7 percent of available resources as against an average of 17.5 percent from 1949 to 1951.' OEEC, *European Economy*, 125.
43. Andreas G. Papandreou, *A Strategy for Economic Development* (Athens, 1962), 18-9.
44. Sweet-Escott, op. cit., 107, 112-13, 193; Candilis, op. cit., 79. For more on how United States foreign policy affects the structural under-development of the Third World see the useful anthology in Fann, K. T. and D. C. Hodges (ed.) *Readings in U.S. Imperialism*, Boston, 1971. Also Andre Gunder Frank. *Latin America: Under-development or Revolution*, New York, 1969.
45. SDNA, 868.50/7-2649, A-471; SDNA, 868.50/9-1649, Office Memo. For more about the Bretton Woods system see A. L. K. Acheson, et. al., eds., *Bretton Woods Revisited* (Toronto: University of Toronto Press, 1972); Edward S. Mason and Robert E. Asher, *The World Bank since Bretton Woods* (Washington, D.C.: The Brookings Institution, 1973). For a critical appraisal of the Bretton Woods system from a marxian perspective see Magdoff, H. *The Age of Imperialism*, New York, 1969, 144-9; Eduardo Galeano, 'Latin America and the Theory of Imperialism', in Fann and Hodges, op. cit., 216-7; and Cheryl Payer, *The Debt Trap: The IMF and the Third World* (New York: Monthly Review Press, 1974), 22-6.
46. OEEC, *Europe the Way Ahead*, 271.

91

47. Angelopoulos, op. cit., 306-7.
48. SDNA, 611.81/11-457, No. 308. For a recent study on United States foreign economic policy and commercial relations with Eastern Europe see Stephen A. Garrett, 'The Economics of American Trade with Eastern Europe: The Carrot or the Stick?' *East European Quarterly* 15 (1981): 485-508.
49. Democratic Organisation of Greece, *Third Blue Book*, 1950, 22.
50. Candilis, op. cit., 52-3.
51. SDNA, 868.5042/12-149, No. 6,991; Katsoulis, op. cit., 6:303; Psyroukis, op. cit., 1:400; Tsoucalas, Constantine, *The Greek Tragedy*, Harmondsworth, 1969, 114; *Third Blue Book*, 124-5; FO 371 RG 1102/9, No. 818; FO 371 RG 1101/1, No. 5.
52. ERP, *Greece*, 28.
53. Agapitidis, op. cit., 243.
54. A. Papandreou, *Economic Development*, 23-5; A. Pepelasis and P. A. Yotopoulos, *Labor Surplus in Greek Agriculture, 1950-1960* (Athens, 1962), 57-66; Angelopoulos, op. cit., 1:295; OEEC, *Europe the Way Ahead*, 271-3.
55. Seton-Watson, op. cit., 335.
56. *Third Blue Book*, 22-3. Sweet-Escott, op. cit., 115; Tsoucalas, op. cit., 129; SDNA, 611.81/10-560, No. 325. For more details about the role of the United States and the Colombian steel mill see FO 371/81492, AL 1101/1, No. 1; FO 371/81492, AL 1300/1300/11, No. 8; Jon V. Kofas, *Dependence and Underdevelopment in Colombia* (Tempe: Center for Latin American Studies), 1986.
57. Cited in Tsoucalas, op. cit., 129.
58. For more details about dumping in Greece see *Third Blue Book*, 25. For a general study on the issue of 'dumping' by the advanced countries see Hamza Alavi and Amir Khurso, 'Pakistan: The Burden of Aid', in R. I. Rhodes, ed., *Imperialism and Underdevelopment* (New York: Monthly Review Press, 1970), 62-77; SDNA, 868.506-2749, A-406; FRUS, 1949, VI, 232; Chandler, Geoffrey, *The Divided Land*, London, 1959, 197-9; FO 371 RG 1011/1, No. 7.
59. Cited in the *Third Blue Book*, 117.
60. Sweet-Escott, op. cit., 155; Candilis, op. cit., 61. SDNA, 868.50/12-149, No. 6,991. For more on the taxation issue see Angelopoulos, op. cit., 1:298-9.
61. Candilis, op. cit., 75.
62. For complete details about Greece's induction into NATO see Theodore A. Couloumbis, *Greek Political Reaction to American and NATO Influences* (New Haven: Yale University Press, 1966), 33-50. For analysis of the Mission's policy directives to the Greek government see McNeill, op. cit., 229; Candilis, op. cit., 53; Sweet-Escott, op. cit., 113-4; OEEC, *European Economy*, 127; FO 371 WG 1011/1, No. 13; FO 371 RG 1101/10, No. 1,095.
63. Cited in *Third Blue Book*, 17, 21.
64. For more concerning Papagos see A. Papandreou, *Democracy at Gunpooint: The Greek Front*, Harmondsworth, 1973, 126-34, Meynaud, op. cit., 93-6; Carey, J. P. C. and A. G. Carey. *The Web of Modern Greek Politics*, London, 1968, 149-57. For more about the devaluation of the drachma and Markezinis' revelations see Sweet-Escott, op. cit., 154; Psyroukis, op. cit., 2:83-4. FO 371 WG 110/5, No. 65E.
65. Kariotis, op. cit., 91-2. It should be noted that in January 1952 the ECA was formally abolished and replaced by the Mutual Security Agency, MSA, whose purpose was solely strategic. See Rubin, *Billion Dollars*, 57-8; Robert A. Packanham, *Liberal America and the Third World* (Princeton: Princeton

University Press, 1973), 49–50; Felix Gilbert, *The End of the European Era, 1890 to the Present* (New York: W. W. Norton and Co., 1984), 432. The Foreign Office declassified documents have revealed that the British government was convinced that American advisers in Athens were in control of the country. See FO 371 RG 1011/1, No. 7; FO 371 RG 1102/3, No. 79; FO 371 WG 1011/1, No. 13; Meynaud, op. cit., 430–31; FO 371 WG 1101/11, No. 161E.

66. Sismanides, S. D. 'Foreign Capital Investment in Greece' in *Balkan Studies* 8 (Summer 1967), 339–52.

67. Ibid., 342–3. A recent study dealing with direct foreign investment in Greece is by A. Gregorogiannis, *To Xeno Kefalaio stin Ellada* (Athens, 1980). This is not a scholarly work and it covers primarily the decade of the 1970s. Nevertheless, it has some useful information on the issue of de-capitalization of Greece. For a broader look at the issue of capital flight from the Third World to the metropolis see Magdoff, op. cit., 155–6; Galeano, 'Imperialism', 217; L. S. Stavrianos, *Global Rift: The Third World Comes of Age* (New York, 1981), 440–56.

ABBREVIATIONS (Footnotes)

AMAG	American Mission for Aid to Greece
ECA	Economic Co-operation Administration
ERP	Economic Recovery Program
FO	Foreign Office
FRUS	Foreign Relations of the United States
GR	GREECE (Official Documents)
OEEC	Organisation for European Economic Co-operation
SDNA	STATE DEPARTMENT. NATIONAL ARCHIVES

Excerpt from the author's recent book. *Intervention and Under-development: Greece during the Cold War*, Pennsylvania State University Press. 1989.

WOMEN IN GREEK SOCIETY

Janet Hart

Editorial Introduction

From antiquity woman has been a powerful — if for many centuries a dormant — presence in the Greek world. One need only recall Homer's delicate one-line psychological portraits of women and, especially in the Odyssey, the traces of a half-recollected matriarchy which led at one time to the theory that this epic might have been the work of a woman. Ancient Greek drama brings us Alcestis and Antigone, figures of towering moral stature, and even the catastrophic figures, such as Clytemnestra and Medea, are vivid, dynamic personalities. Indeed a choric ode from Euripides' Medea, in the late Gilbert Murray's verse translation, was used as a battle-hymn by British Suffragettes. In classical Athens women's position was by no means a good one but even the oligarchic Plato gave women an equal position amongst the rulers of his ideal state.

The later religions of the Near East, Christianity, but more especially the nearly four centuries of Moslem Ottoman rule reduced Greek woman to the status of a chattel, but she still bore the brunt of the mainly agricultural work and, when occasion demanded, she could show her worth like the heroines of the 1821–32 Greek Independence struggle, Bubulina and Mado Mavrogenous. Nevertheless, in the early years of this century, her position was such that a provincial judge could acquit a rapist because his unmarried victim was illegitimate and therefore 'no man's property'.

Janet Hart shows us how and why this position has changed rapidly since the Second World War and, basically, for the same reason that British women's contribution during the First World War brought to fruition the campaign for women's suffrage. In this case it was women's participation in and contribution to the wartime Resistance. Greece can now be said to have caught up. Women members of parliament (even a deputy-speaker), MEPs, a woman EEC Commissioner, women provincial prefects and elected women mayors are now a familiar feature of the Greek scene.

In the contemporary period, the changing status of women in Greece can best be understood in terms of the two phases most often used to examine 20th century American and European women's history: 'first wave' and 'second wave' feminism. These categories will hopefully serve to clarify *both* important mass developments *and* the role played by indigenous Greek feminist movements and organizations. The term 'first wave feminism' refers to the initial stages of the incorporation of women into a political system and according to the usual model, culminates in women being extended the basic citizenship right of suffrage.[1] 'Second wave feminism' applies to 'the women's movements which sprang up almost simultaneously in the late 1960s and 1970s in advanced capitalist societies (that in spite of local variations) were clearly the product of massive and rapid alterations in the position of women in post-war society'.[2] My purpose here will be to discuss women's changing social, political and legal positions in Greece according to this more universally understood framework, but also to underscore those aspects of the case that are uniquely Greek. For in Greece, undoubtedly the most important aspect of the *first wave of feminism* is that, paradoxically, women participated in the National Resistance (Ethniki Antistasi) from 1941–44, and that in the years from 1945–65, the ideological consequences of those activities were a mixed blend of empowerment and repression. *Second wave feminism* in Greece encompasses resistance to the dictatorship from 1967 to 1974 and the role played by women in anti-junta organizations both abroad and underground which later became the basis of the modern women's movement in Greece; and the reforms which have been instituted more recently, especially the Family Law Bill. The latter was passed in 1983 under the PASOK government, even though, in many ways, public opinion had already shifted in favour of the new legislation.

Eternal Rules She Disregards:[3] Greek Women in Resistance and First Wave Feminism

'The moment the Germans left Vaphe with our operator, Elpida quickly took the wireless and the other incriminating things a little way off, and hid them; conducting herself, although she was a woman, with all the sense and coolness of a brave man.'[4]

'But the one he had most enjoyed writing, he said, was an anti-feminist poem satirizing the women who, during the previous particularly bitter winter, had worn men's trousers to protect themselves from the cold when engaged in olive picking in the fields.'[5]

One purpose of this paper is to offer alternative and more specific models of women's political development in transitional societies, or those which, like Greece, exhibit a combination of Western and non-Western traits. In England and the United States, the usually incremental (and often not directly linear) process of women's empowerment within the socio-political system was initiated by the suffrage movement. In China, 'female solidarity groups' inaugurated by the Communist Party in the 1930s were the main vehicles used to encourage the participation of women (Croll, 1979). During the 1920s in Israel, women's agricultural collectives played a role in this process (Izraeli, 1981). In India, it has been asserted, an important political by-product of the nationalist movement was the introduction of women into political life. That movement provided an ideological framework for Indian women to begin to gain a small measure of power and influence in the national political arena in contrast to what they had before. In Greece, I will contend, this process was initiated, not by a suffrage movement, nor by labour organizations or agricultural cooperatives, but — closer to the Indian model — by the resistance movement. The data I have collected[6] show that a politically significant number of women were mobilized into the Greek resistance movement beginning in 1941 and especially into the largest organization, the EAM,[7] because a mass-based social movement was being created simultaneously within the movement whose original purpose was to resist Nazi occupation. The underlying purpose of the social movement was to incorporate certain groups into the political system whose social status and public visibility were low, or who were disfranchised altogether.

For purposes of analysis, I separate the movement for resistance to the occupation and the social movement into two distinct entities. However, the social movement cannot really be considered to be an isolated phenomenon with a life of its own. It was never formally christened 'The Greek Women's Emancipation Movement'. Its membership did not primarily consist of activists and it did not employ protest tactics to agitate for women's rights. But in a more oblique manner, it denoted a series of acts aimed at another sort of resistance: resistance to a set of cultural and political rules of conduct that effectively barred women. This secondary movement provided a means for women to upgrade their low status in the society by making a shift from what some feminist writers have seen as the greatly undervalued private sphere to the more prestigious public sphere (Rosaldo, 1974; Elshtain, 1981). Even those women who didn't consciously perceive the movement as a vehicle for social advancement nonetheless stood to benefit inadvertently. The movement that started out to mobilize civilians purely for resistance to the Nazis was transformed into a progressive social movement, particularly as far as its major organizational branch was concerned. Explanations for this political development can be found in a) the psychological receptiveness of the women themselves to empowerment; b) the organizational strategies of the EAM leadership, especially those sympathetic to 'the woman question'; and c) the political vacuum left when the Greek government relocated to Cairo on Axis Occupation. The resistance, I will argue, actively facilitated the liberation of its female participants in a relative sense, by providing a legitimate yet revolutionary method of social change.

EAM's membership was broad. It included all socio-economic classes (with a notably large middle-class component)[8] and ages, from children and teenagers to the elderly. With its Communist-oriented philosophy of mass organization, EAM hoped to mobilize a cross-section of the population in each occupied zone (German, Italian, Bulgarian), including those who in some sense had been 'left out' of the political system. Besides women, this category included youth, villagers, and the Asia Minor refugees who had faced considerable prejudice since their arrival from Turkey in great numbers after the 1922 Asia Minor Disaster.[9] Since EAM was the largest resistance organization,[10] and women were a key target of its overall mobilization strategy, that cluster of organizations inevitably had the most far-reaching effects for Greek women. However, other smaller organizations such as PEAN[11] in Athens also included many heroic women and girls who by participating in the resistance were for the first time defying the rigid standards of conduct that the patriarchal social structure of Greece had in the past demanded of them.

Indeed, in the period prior to the resistance, Greek women were afforded very little personal freedom in the public sphere; a situation that differed little from that which prevailed in many other countries at the time, but one that was aggravated by the primarily agrarian, dependent character of its economy, its geographical isolation, and by the traditional weakness of movements such as labour and suffrage.[12] In France, England and Germany, for example, these movements served, if not to accomplish full reform, then to activate public opinion and to place the concerns of their members on the political agenda. Supplementing the legal and social constraints placed on women were a number of cultural notions originating from a mixture of mythology, tradition, and Orthodox religion, some of which, as criticized by Plato in the 4th century B.C.,[13] were long-entrenched features of social and political discourse about women. Based on these Weberian-style ideal types, women were unreliable, irresponsible, and, like Eve, easily seduced if left to their own devices. Females were thought to be most efficient and trustworthy when fulfilling their responsibilities within the home, in spite of evidence that in many rural areas, women laboured under the 'double burden' of maintaining both the house and the family fields (Friedl, 1962; DuBoulay, 1974, 1986; Dubisch, 1986). Duties involving public contact were to be kept to a minimum; and to be dispatched meekly and without undue ceremony. 'Unmarried girls on an errand,' writes Campbell, 'should walk briskly. Those who habitually loiter on corners, and look around, endanger their reputations.'[14]

When Axis troops invaded Greece in April 1941 and later

when actual resistance organizations were formed, the Pindus mountain women who had carried supplies loaded on their backs to Greek forces in Albania were legendary. Similarly, women played a well-publicized role in the Battle of Crete (April–May, 1941) with Cretan regulars caught on the mainland in the process of being evacuated from the Albanian front. During the winter of 1941–42, an estimated 300,000 Greek citizens starved to death due to food shortages brought on by massive requisitioning on behalf of the occupying forces. Women were the main organizers of the soup kitchens that kept the death toll from being higher.

During the early period of spontaneous popular uprising, women were active primarily through the traditional support functions such as cooking, cleaning, and sheltering (of escaping British troops). These traditional roles were only adapted and extended when the men were absent. But as the war progressed, and with the advent of an organized resistance, women and girls began to undertake more radical activities. They were recruited into specific organizations and began to commit acts of sabotage that were punishable by death or imprisonment. In Athens, this was particularly true of the youth organizations, EPON and PEAN. In the countryside, where EAM had recruited whole villages, married, widowed and elderly women also engaged in a wider range of activities, and at great personal risk. With the advent of an at first scattered and later more concerted resistance to German occupation, then, many of the deeply-imbedded visions of a woman's proper role were laid aside for pragmatic reasons. Greece faced the threat of an outside enemy and the reality of war. More specifically, the 'fighting spirit' was fuelled by the intense nationalism that has long been part of Greek political culture[15] and which cut across all societal divisions, the widely-publicized victories of Greek forces against the Italians in Albania, and the heart-felt resentment of many Greeks to the fascist dictatorship of General Metaxas which had existed on Greek soil since 1936. Thus, for the first time, girls who were not allowed even to talk to a man in public were mobilized into resistance organizations and were sent on dangerous missions. Some, between the tender ages of 14 and 20, were running guns, spying, or 'had a price on their heads'.[16] Thus, by 1944, approximately one third[17] of all Greek women had probably engaged in some kind of resistance activity. In 1943 and 1944, particularly, a number of women such as Lela Karayianni[18] and, for example, 187 women from the village of Katranitsa[19] were shot by the Germans in reprisals and so-called 'liquidation operations', each winning the right to become what a later song about a 'palikari' or brave young man would refer to as 'a red lily of the field'. Others, like Electra Apostolou, were tortured to death in Nazi prisons rather than disclose names and details connected with the resistance to German authorities.[20]

During the resistance period, with the Greek government operating *in absentia* from the Middle East, the EAM–ELAS organization had in C. M. Woodhouse's words 'acquired control of almost the whole country'.[21] That organization was consequently exempted from having to answer to either the old political guard or the monarch in making policy and was in a legitimate position to adjust public cultural and political attitudes. Although it would be an exaggeration to claim complete success for EAM's policy with regard to women at the 'rank-and-file' level, nevertheless the trend initiated by the organization was generally inclusive and sensitive to women's plight. To a degree, the sincerity of EAM/ELAS leaders about the need to counter age-old social barriers may only be speculated, since most of these innovators are no longer available for comment and the actual minutes of wartime strategy sessions are scarce. However, indirect evidence of the priority placed on expanding female membership and reorienting public belief systems can be discerned in a number of pragmatic attempts at reform. For example, the intricate *katharevoussa*, the formal Greek language spoken and read by the educated elite, was replaced by the more widely-used *demotic* Greek for official resistance business and publications. The importance of this gesture was considerable, both politically and symbolically. The overall effect was to broaden the circles of communication to encompass much of the country's marginalized population, including many peasants and women previously not conversant in the ceremonious *katharevoussa*. A further indication of the leadership's avowed interest in challenging traditional attitudes was the organization of a Theatre of the Mountains under the aegis of Vasilis Rotas[22] in 1942. Troupes of actors and singers travelled around the countryside; among other duties, these players were charged with recruiting women and girls and with performing skits in which, for example, a character would denounce his wife, claiming that she was stupid and inferior. In the denouement, his remarks would be exposed and ridiculed, as members of the village audience jeered and stamped their feet along with the rest of the cast.

In addition to breaking through entrenched cultural stereotypes about women, a number of more formal political rights were bestowed. The most significant was the right to vote and the equal rights clause that appeared in the PEEA constitution in the spring of 1944.[23] And while in ELAS women had mainly fought in separate women's units, in the Democratic Army of the civil war period they often appear to have fought side-by-side with the men, even rising to the command of mixed units in certain areas. One of the most surprising photographs of the 1940s, taken by Spiros Meletzis, shows a woman in an ELAS uniform demonstrating the use of a rifle to an attentive group of men.

It is difficult to imagine, from the perspective of a society which now takes women's suffrage for granted and has been conditioned by the tenets of the modern women's movement, what these changes meant to the Greek women who experienced them. The resistance affected not only its female activists, but also provided plausible role models for those who could not participate so readily. Perhaps the most moving account of what the changes wrought by the EAM organization, and what participation in the general phenomena of resistance meant to these women and girls, is best expressed in their own words. For example, a youth organizer comments:

'I remember that we girls, in school, we had, how would one put it? . . . a disadvantage, because we had strict rules at home, because the boys were freer, because young women weren't allowed to pursue an education the way the boys could. That is, a girl finishing high school could only stay at home. Whereas a boy could go on to the university to study . . . In the spring of 1942, an organization called EAM Youth was formed. The reason it was formed was that, well, at that time, girls' chances of being able to join a mixed organization were very slim. Their mentality, the preconceptions, the difficulties they would encounter at home . . . that was the most important thing . . . that is, they would first of all have problems at home, because they would be in the company of boys. Girls had very tight restrictions. Secondly, women, because they were so sheltered, it would have been much more difficult for them to gain any sort of recognition, to be heard, to be able to grow and change at all when among the men. The men "covered them over" with their dynamism, with the confidence which comes from having some leeway in society, with their experience, they were involved in politics, in everything. So this organization was concerned with helping girls to have the courage to speak up, to not be so hesitant. It covered both of these problems. The ones that the girls would face at home, and the problems that had to do with timidity. Thousands of girls were mobilized into this organization in Athens. It was a big step.'[24]

In a recent documentary film on the subject, an elderly village woman says,

'I remember that the government made beautiful things happen, and we were raised to a higher level. The other governments had neglected the peasants. Beautiful things happened, like voting. I voted. And we helped in the local government in any way we could.'[25]

A woman from a working class neighbourhood of Athens says,

'In the resistance, I learned to love books and other people's rights. Actually, it created my whole character, because, remember, I was just a child in the beginning . . . The women's movement today is not as it was before — the resistance got women out of their homes to work for society.'[26]

A woman from Kozani (north central Greece) says,

'In the old days in the villages, it was considered shameful for a woman to work. They would say to you "You don't have any money to live and that's why you put your daughter to work!" It was an embarrassment. And besides that, for the most part they never sent them to school. You would go until the dimotiko (primary school), you would know how to read, count, and write, and that was enough. Then they'd say, "Get back in the house, to wash the dishes and sweep the floor." That was the role of the woman. For those of us who were at the point of deciding what to do with our lives, the resistance changed all that . . .'[27]

A woman from an upper-class Athenian neighbourhood says,

'(Politically), Greece had been divided in half, let's say, as Greece has always been divided in two. And at that time, the EAM . . . well, the other organizations, the rightist ones, were much smaller in strength and number, and most people went with EAM, and with EPON, that was for the young people . . . but all of that "sat on our heads like a hat". We weren't at all interested in either the names or who was behind all of it, and it was really by chance and circumstances that we ended up in that organization and not in another. But of course, my friends and I were in support of the poor people, and those wronged by society, and we wanted a kind of social justice to reign — therefore there is really no doubt that we were of the left. But at that time, they didn't know that Communism was connected with EAM, that is, most people weren't Communists in the least, they were simply what we call "Left" (aristeros). Aristeros, what does that mean? That is to say, with a social conscience, for some kind of justice to exist, that people should not be oppressed by people with more power . . . of course, we didn't really know much about the details, since we were very young, 15, 16, 17 years old, what did we know about politics? We were active only to show our dislike of the occupying forces. Naturally, we didn't tell our parents that we were in EPON because they would've been so worried for our safety, and that's why my father was so shocked when the Germans came and they knocked on our door at four in the morning, and then he said to them, "I am her father and please take me and not my daughter, who's just a little girl".[28]

"And another thing, because we were so hungry, there was a lot of activity around that. There was a path that went through a field across from our house and we would use it to go get bread at the bakery, you know, the kind of bread they would give us then, that horrible stuff that had wood-shavings in it, and all anyone got of it was just a handful of pieces. And there, the Germans had their cars lined up all along the length of the field, from the road over to where we would go to the bakery. One morning, I saw that the bonnet of the engine of one of the trucks was lifted. Why no one was around, I have no idea. And I said to myself, "I should sabotage them!". I thought of it on my own and I went back to the house and I got a pair of pliers and I came back and stuck my hand in. Fortunately, my hand didn't reach the wires because it was very far; otherwise, I was prepared to cut the wires of the engine! I tell you, people were crazy!! The point is, we weren't afraid! We were so . . . how can I put it? We weren't the least bit worried that we would be killed, we didn't think about being caught . . . we had absolutely no reservations about what we were doing.'[29]

A woman from a mountain village near Karpenissi, says:

'Why did I join the resistance? Eh, at that time, of course, there were the conquerors (the *kataktites*) in our country, and we knew who the conquerors were, Hitler, the Axis, the Fascists . . . and we knew that if we didn't fight, we wouldn't be able to throw out the *kataktites*. Besides that, we also had fascism on our soil too, we had the Metaxas dictatorship, and that had to change . . . And, the developments for us personally . . . as I told you, for women, it was a chance to make things better.'[30]

A woman from Chania, Crete, says:

'Look. If the resistance hadn't come along, well, my father had a high social position and was a very successful businessman . . . I don't know if I would have stayed in school, because you know the mentality in the villages, well, conservative, that is, "You're already 20", they would say to you, "you'd better get married". Eh, we would've had a life, well, different, let's say.'[31]

Another woman from Chania, says:

'At that time there wasn't . . . women couldn't really go outside much, we couldn't be out at night, no, no . . . but after the resistance, and with what it had created, the woman came out of her house. That is, before, in the house, you had to always be in the house; for girls, our path ran only between school and the house. If we were going somewhere, we would go with our father, with our brother, we weren't even allowed to go anywhere in a group, do you understand? And the married woman: in the house. Neither work, nor any wandering around was tolerated. There were women who were teachers,[32] but they were few in number before the occupation. But after the resistance, after the occupation, when the woman came out of the house, she was more liberated, let's say, and she became more creative . . . And that's what began the fight for the equality of women. And for the vote, and all of that . . . because we didn't have any of that before.'[33]

Finally, a woman from a small, right-wing resistance organization, says:

'My parents didn't know about my activity, and I hid all my documents in my granny's drawer under her underwear. She was blind, and couldn't hear too well and my parents almost never checked her room. My parents often said, "A girl should be tended like a hothouse flower" and that's exactly how I felt, because we had a little green-house where I used to spend a lot of time doing my lessons and embroidering. I think now, looking back, that my greatest resistance was not on the streets of Athens, but at home.'[34]

A Fruit of Unripe Wisdom:[35] First Wave Feminism Dismantled, 1944–64

Ultimately, the 'women's movement' that was embedded in the resistance was unable to fulfill its promise. During the Civil War (1946–49) and the 1950s, female resistance participants were demobilized as a result of the return to exclusionary politics after the war, accompanied by a reversal of the wartime public ideology favourable to women's participation. However, based on the oral evidence, I maintain that the effects of women playing a more active role in political life, and, more generally, in the public sphere, were never completely erased because of the way in which the EAM mobilized women during a period when the central political institutions of the country were particularly vulnerable to change. Furthermore, the lessons in confidence and personal power that the resistance provided the women and girls who either joined or had some contact with the resistance, were invaluable. Strong traces of the reorienting influence of the resistance on women activists can most notably be found in the life histories of those women who became political prisoners during the Civil War.

By the end of 1944, the 'White Terror', aimed at Communists and former partisans was in full swing. Many EAM leaders, members, and their relatives were arrested and sent to jails and concentration camps. Former EAM members and their families were pursued by extreme right-wing terrorist bands. The resistance turned progressive movement was thus demobilized by state-administered and sanctioned repression during the late 1940s and throughout the 1950s. A successful record of mass mobilization was no match for the political stigma of Communism in the post-war era. Anyone associated with EAM was the possible target of remnants of the 'tagmatasfalites' (Security Battalions), wartime collaborators trained by the Nazis to counter the resistance, and of roving parastate groups. Both were strongly influenced by the Greek government's anti-Communist ideology and in the midst of the Cold War, often supplied with American weapons.[36]

An Example: The Women of the Averoff
Among the casualties of this counter-movement were the newly-emancipated women who took part in the resistance along with the female relatives of EAM members. Rapes and killings reached ghoulish proportions. For example, in the women's section of the Averoff Prison, seventeen executions were carried out in 1948 and 1949. The youngest was 16 years old.[37] But while the movement's political and social achievements were seriously damaged, they were not completely reversed. New modes of collective action were employed by jailed activists and their relatives, by under-

ground groups, and within the EDA party, the only legal political alternative on the Left from 1951 to 1967. The women of the Trikeri and Makronisos island exile camps, of the Averoff Prison in Athens, of the Patras and Kerkyra (Corfu) prisons, and of other regional detention centres sustained a type of collective action that was not, as might be expected, blatantly political. Survivors of these difficult times say that their resistance activity provided a clear motivation to survive.

For example, one of the symbolically most important groups among the female political prisoners that the Greek Civil War created was the aforementioned women of the Averoff Prison in Athens. Many spent from 1 to 15 years in prison.[38] However, as a result of the repressive post-war political climate, very little hard data exists on these women. They were considered to be 'dangerous to the public welfare' (epikindines) and 'official enemies of the State and the Greek family' until after 1974. Questions of how and why the women of the Averoff resisted torture and the continual pressure to sign statements of repentance renouncing their resistance activity (diloseis), remain unanswered. My data indicate that two key factors contributed to the remarkable stamina of the women of the Averoff. The first is that the organization *cum* guiding ideology of the EAM created a kind of 'resistance momentum' that helped sustain these women through the hard times. This spirit of resistance continued to be fuelled by their common experiences and decisions in prison. Secondly, the group of prisoners (at one time numbering as many as 500 women) were fairly representative in terms of age, region, and socio-economic class. A kind of social microcosm was formed that gave these women living proof that the participatory ideals fostered by the resistance could be carried out in practice.

In examining the case of the women of the Averoff, we can observe several kinds of resistance strategies of the type that were employed in jails, prisons and island exile camps all over Greece. Most impressively, these tactics were *collectively* conceived during the early period from 1947–49, when most of the long-term detainees were arrested and when seventeen women were executed (1948 and 1949). The main such types of activity were:

1. The refusal to sign statements of repentance (diloseis) even if it meant death. Those selected for execution would not show fear, in order to give the others courage and to make a statement to the jailers.
2. Singing and dancing around the large palm tree in the prison courtyard (the finikas) along with the condemned woman on the eve of her execution.
3. Lessons were arranged in the areas of expertise of the incarcerated teachers, e.g. literacy, French, mathematics, literature, classics. A singing group was organized and makeshift plays, usually of classical works and myths written by inmates, were performed.
4. Responsibilities were divided and delegated to various inmate committees, in the areas of, for example, cleanliness, package distribution, recreation/amusement (psyhagogia).

One woman, who at the age of 15 was sentenced to death and was released from prison 14 years later, says:

'In jail, we had a kind of socialism. Packages from home would come for us with food, with clothes, and they would all be gathered in one place and the goods would be distributed to those who needed them, privately, by our own prisoner committees. I never would know exactly what my family had brought me. Many times, though, they (the distribution committee) would tell us the specifics so we knew what to thank our families for; and there were women who designated what would go where, that is, this will go to someone who is sick, that needs it, this will go to the youngest girls who need it to grow, this will go to the elderly women who no longer have good teeth to chew because it's soft . . . and to women whose families lived far away or were dead and couldn't send them things, or for the children that were inside with their mothers.'[39]

Repression in Context

More generally, one can say that the repressive tactics used to demobilize EAM were particularly effective in the Greek context. The formal aspects of political displacement of the Left during this period are, by now, fairly obvious. EAM leaders and members were exterminated, exiled, or imprisoned in a manner which Constantine Tsoucalas has written 'can only be compared with the sombre fate of the Spanish intelligentsia' under Franco.[40] Once released from prison, most were obliged to check in with the Security Police at regular intervals, sometimes weekly. With the Communist and Socialist parties outlawed, the only legal alternative was the EDA (United Democratic Left) party, whose influence in the political arena was negligible. Mobilized women who had not fled or been sent to prison were left with the options of: a) joining the EDA (which had a women's organization); b) working in underground organizations; or c) bowing out of politics altogether.

But at the cultural and ideological levels, the effects were no less debilitating. The social consequences of such open humiliation were enormous, particularly in light of the pivotal role that honour (timi) played in an individual extended family member's dealing with outsiders. A tarnished reputation meant social ostracism. Thus, during the 1950s, the publication of the family name in a regional newspaper in connection with political 'crimes against the State' could mean that even a person who was a child during the resistance might later be denied a job or be singled out at school. For women and girls, whose world, in spite of the resistance still revolved around building and nurturing a family, one purpose these tactics served was to equate participation in the movement with moral degeneracy. A good family name and irreproachable conduct were especially vital to girls of marriageable age. The institution of the dowry was in full swing.[41] Participation in EPON and/or subsequent imprisonment, for instance, could call a young woman's virginity into question, an important part of an honourably drawn-up marriage contract. Post-war propaganda suggested that women in the EAM organizations had spent the war engaged in prostitution. For example, a song called 'To the EPONitisses' (girls of EPON) and sung by parastate groups, claims:

> 'Now that the Germans are here,
> your belly is flat
> and when the Russians come
> your belly will grow
> Babies and many other gifts
> the Greek mountains give you
> with swollen bellies and
> your string of cartridges
> *you* are the heroines of ELAS.'[42]

As a result of repressive techniques that were well-grounded in local social realities, the general message given to women and girls during the 20-year period that followed liberation was that their most legitimate life-choice was to return home and stay there. This was, not coincidentally, in keeping with the philosophy that sent Rosie the Riveter out of the factory and back to the kitchen in the post-war era in the United States. Mobilization had raised women's expectations regarding the expanded role they might play in the public sphere. One goal of demobilization was to deflate these expectations and to reinstate more traditional lifestyles for women.

However, it must be emphasized that this goal was in part supplanted by a new trend, one that was certainly not unique to Greece, as European economies began to expand. Increasingly, women began to work outside the home, if not in the villages, then at least in Athens, Salonica, and the larger regional towns. The phenomenon of post-war urbanization in Greece would eventually result in an approximately 30% increase in the number of Greeks residing in cities. It became much more usual than in the past for a girl with secondary education to take a job upon leaving school or to attend university. Often those who married either wanted to or were compelled by the family's economic situation to continue working. This dilemma was eased somewhat by the presence in many Greek households of, typically, a widowed grandmother eager to undertake the responsibilities of child-care.

Despite the repression of the civil war years, a Centre Government led by General Plastiras took office in 1950 and 'pacification measures' were introduced which gradually emptied the concentration camps, beginning with the women. Among its last reconstructive acts, this Government gave the vote to women in March 1952 and women hurried to register. But in the November 1952 elections, when the conservative Greek Rally party under Field-Marshal Papagos defeated the divided Centre and Left, women did not actually vote because the registers were not yet ready.

Since the majority system was in use at that time, January 1953 produced a by-election in Salonica and the new left party EDA put up its chairman, an extremely popular local gynaecologist who had delivered more than one generation of Salonica's infants. Alarmed at the possible weight of the new and incalculable women's vote, the conservative party put up a competing candidate who, after a closely-contested election, became the first woman member of the Greek parliament. Although she left a barely legible mark on Greek history and it is doubtful if today anyone even remembers her name, all parties now began to develop women's sections and to train women as political workers. Since women voted in separate polling booths, this also led to the need for female election agents capable of supervising the polling. At first, politically-conscious actresses were the usual choice for this job, as it was thought that only they would display the necessary toughness. The 1956 elections produced a small number of women members of parliament, including Vaso Thanasekou of EDA.[43]

Conclusion

The type of mobilization initiated by the resistance movement created new political networks and provided individual incentives for women to continue their participation in the public realm. Younger women who had been members of the centre-right organizations now conceived of their life chances differently. Those women who were no longer politically active gained enough confidence to stay out of the shadows. Although the number of active women declined dramatically, the resistance left an important ideological impression on the political system. For instance, in 1952, as mentioned above, women were given the vote. Although this move was probably mostly for reasons of political expediency, nevertheless it showed that women had, for the first time, been discerned as a political constituency. In this sense, the resistance can be seen as a kind of indigenous suffrage movement, a harbinger of hellenic first wave feminism. An observer of the situation in the United States after 1920 notes that 'the social, economic, and political separation that had encouraged different ways of thinking, that had given plausibility to the assertion that innate psychological differences between the sexes were so great that women must be kept in their customary sphere, melted away. Disfranchisement itself had bred differences in thinking and social roles between enfranchised and disfranchised that had provided arguments for maintaining their political separation'.[44] Thus, in much the same way that the achievement of the principal goals of the suffrage movement did not rule out further setbacks for British and American women and by no means insured the end of sex discrimination, the resistance movement did not suddenly make Greek women equal with Greek men. Still, its ideological effects were novel, and to a large degree, irreversible.

The International Dimension: Second Wave Feminism in Greece, the 1970s and '80s

In 1963, Betty Friedan published her path-breaking book expressing the sense of oppression that European and American women would later make the basis of the modern women's movement. In fact, writers such as Friedan and Simone de Beauvoir[45] were among the first in the modern era to point out basic inequities in the female condition, their ideas bearing a close similarity to what Mary Wollstonecraft and others of the Lockeian school had written nearly two centuries before.[46] The common thread running through both clusters of feminist thought, although written in vastly different eras, was that women should be allowed, like men, to develop themselves to their fullest potential instead of being closetted away and consistently under-educated and undervalued. In *The Feminine Mystique*, Friedan used popular women's magazines and interviews to unearth a striking paradox: that American women in the post-war era were being told by the media to fit the image of the happy housewife and yet, all too often, this life seemed to result in frustration, anxiety and substance abuse. 'Millions of wives and mothers nursed a secret, guilty misery which she labelled "the problem that has no name". Lived in reality, the life of the "happy housewife" . . . offer(ed) no sense of independence, identity or achievement.'[47] Interviews with women, psychologists, and social scientists revealed that women felt very keenly that there were no alternatives to this isolated existence.

Friedan saw the problem as having both cultural and political dimensions. Not only did the image of 'the feminine mystique' need to be altered; women must also struggle for increased political rights and power. Later, circa 1967, American and European women began to organize and openly protest their oppression in what was now termed 'the women's movement'. This movement became even more radical when women's groups were formed in the context of the student movement. In protest against perceived discriminatory treatment within their organizations by the same men who advocated a more general revolution based on social equality, university women broke off and formed their own consciousness-raising groups in the US, Britain, France and Italy (Jenson, 1983; Ergas, 1979, 1985).

In the late 1960s and early 1970s, when the modern women's movement was beginning elsewhere, Greece was ruled by a military dictatorship. From 1967 to 1974, all political associations and parties were banned. The Greek women's movement thus began furtively, and its initial structure was fragmented. The struggle for women's rights was subsumed in the more urgent battle to rid Greece of the junta. Many women were among those arrested, exiled, and tortured. Co-ed cells of students protested and worked in underground presses and ferried messages of resistance.

The Greek women's movement was as a result forced to acquire an international dimension during its second phase. Those who had joined the ranks of the diaspora Greeks in order to escape the colonels' regime took note of the new political currents that were surfacing abroad. Many who returned when the dictatorship fell in 1974 brought these innovative ideas back with them and, as the '70s progressed, concerned themselves with blending national and international ideas to fit Greek reality.

A detailed analysis of the course of the Greek women's movement since 1975 is beyond the scope of this paper.[48] However, from a juridical point of view, two key aspects of Greek *second wave feminism* must be mentioned: the equal rights clause which appears in the 1975 Constitution and Greece's very progressive Family Law Bill. I will take one step further into as yet uncharted territory. Namely, I would like to suggest that one reason that the debate about the Family Law Bill was not as bitterly controversial as might have been expected, despite the fact that it was in part addressing crusty old anachronisms that were no longer deemed valid or necessary, is that the resistance *cum* women's movement of the 1940s had left a residue of political consciousness in the generation that lived it. Although 'the truth' of the matter may never really be ascertained, it is here that the links between *first wave feminism* and *second wave feminism* can be seen most clearly in their Greek colorations.

As reported in the July 30th Bulletin of Actions and Decisions of the PEEA (Government of the Mountains) on May 27, 1944, the first Greek equal rights clause was put to a vote and approved. According to Article 5 of the PEEA constitution, 'All Greeks, men and women, have equal political and civil rights.' Since the Government of the Mountains was the legal articulation of EAM's vision of the post-war Greek political system, it is fair to assume that the practice of incorporating women into the political system would have a major priority had the authors of that constitution retained any power after the war and in general, had things not turned out quite differently. Thus, one woman comments,

'After the war, we expected equal relations to continue – we wanted a "people's government" like they had created in the mountains.'[49]

After liberation, anxious not to lose valued legal prerogatives and to fight the misogynous attitudes that were part of the increasingly repressive climate after the war,[50] the first Panhellenic Women's Conference was held in Athens from the 26th through the 29th May, 1946. Delegates from newly-formed women's groups from villages and towns all over Greece attended this convention, including Maria Svolou, a member of the Ruling Council of the Government of the Mountains, and Rosa Imvrioti, a prominent educationalist and member of EAM during the resistance.[51] A primary result of the conference was that the struggle for women's rights was emphasised and the importance of women drawing together and cooperating on a national scale was recognized.

In a practical sense, the issues raised by the 1944 PEEA Constitution and the 1946 Panhellenic Women's Convention were not to play such a pre-eminent part in national politics for another thirty years, until after the fall of the colonels. Article 4, paragraph 2 of the 1975 Greek Constitution reads 'Greek men and Greek women have the same rights and obligations', its wording a striking reminder of the 1944 law. Around the same time, women's groups began to form and, supported by a sense of popular dignity that had long been absent, the discourse about women's role in politics and society was renewed.

A full legal analysis of the complex Family Law Bill is not possible here and would not yield many specific bridges with what might be called 'wartime domestic policy' regarding women's rights. But a spiritual connection with the type of society that the resistance had endeavoured to establish in another era is clearly evident, especially in Articles 1387 and 1510, which abolish the former 'male head of household' stipulation. In the past, the husband was in effect designated 'family monarch' and as such, he possessed the sole and ultimate right to decide on all conjugal matters. According to the 1982 law, such decisions are now made jointly. Children are now under 'parental care' and marital partners are co-responsible for financial and practical questions. The law also officially abolishes the institution of the dowry. The PASOK government has very deliberately, although not necessarily consciously, continued the policy directions originated by EAM with regard to women.[52]

The impact of women's participation in the resistance can clearly be seen in the attitudes of the women who took an active part in the struggle against fascism in the 1940s. It is also evident in the attitudes of some of the men who were in the resistance, particularly toward their wives and about their daughters; in subsequent formal policy changes, such as the 1975 Constitution and the Family Law Bill; and in the fact that in all branches of the otherwise disunified women's movement, female partisans are a symbol of Greek women at their best. The resistance altered assumptions about the mobilizational capacity and potential of women. Today, the contributions of women to the resistance movement are, admittedly, most often vocalized in the language of a uniquely Greek feminism. Yet to a remarkable degree, their participation also changed the Greek political system and, even during what a recent film calls 'The Stone Years', had an inspirational effect on public consciousness.

NOTES

1. See, for example, Janet Saltzman Chafetz and Anthony Dworkin, *Female Revolt: Women's Movement in World and Historical Perspective*, Rowman and Allanheld, 1986; Olive Banks, *Becoming a Feminist: The Social Origins of 'First Wave' Feminism*, University of Georgia Press, 1987; Jane Rendall, *The Origins of Modern Feminism: Women in Britain, France, and the United States*, MacMillan Publishers, 1984; Aileen Kraditor, *The Ideas of the Woman Suffrage Movement, 1890-1920*, (W. W. Norton: 1981) Columbia

University Press, 1985.

2. See Jane Jenson, 'The Modern Women's Movement in Italy, France, and Great Britain: Differences in Life Cycles', in *Comparative Social Research*, Volume 5, pp. 341–375, 1982.

3. From Chin P'ing Mei, *The Adventurous History of Hsi Men and His Six Wives*, written in 17th c. China and quoted in Sheila Rowbotham, *Women, Resistance and Revolution*, Penguin Books, 1972, p. 171.

4. Psychoundakis, George, *The Cretan Runner*, John Murray, London, 1955, p. 91.

5. Ibid., p. 7.

6. Janet C. Hart, 'Empowerment and Political Opportunity: Greek Women in Resistance, 1940–64', Doctoral dissertation, Department of Government, Cornell University, Ithaca, N.Y. Based on field work in Greece from 1983–85, supported by a Fulbright Research Grant. Includes interviews with resistance participants from organizations across the political spectrum (EAM, ELAS, EPON, EDES, RAN, PEAN, and an SOE liaison spy network).

7. EAM (The National Liberation Front) was founded in September 1941, and was loosely tied to the small pre-war Communist Party of Greece. Initially, the influence of the latter was most evident in EAM's mass organizational strategies and to some extent in the leadership stratum, since a majority of EAM's founding members were also members of the Party's Central Committee. Its military branch was called ELAS (The Greek People's Liberation Army), its youth organization was EPON (National Panhellenic Youth Organization), and its welfare organization, staffed mainly by women, was called EA (National Solidarity). The standard membership figure for EAM is 1.5 million out of a population of approximately 7 million in 1940. This estimate refers to participants who were 'ready to lay their lives on the line', and is probably conservative. The other main resistance organization was called EDES (National Greek Republican League). Led by Napoleon Zervas, EDES was initially a republican organization but later became aligned with the Greek monarchy and the British Foreign Office. It was formally inaugurated in September, 1942.

8. See John Louis Hondros, *Occupation and Resistance: The Greek Agony, 1941–44*, Pella Press, New York, 1983, especially Ch. 4, p. 120.

9. See, for example, George Mavrogordatos, *Social Coalitions and Party Strategies in Greece, 1922–36*, University of California–Berkeley Press, 1983.

10. See John L. Hondros, 'The Greek Resistance, 1941–44: A Re-evaluation', in *Greece in the 1940s: A Nation in Crisis*, University Press of New England, 1981, pp. 37–47.

11. The acronym 'PEAN' stood for 'Panellinia Enosi Agonizomenon Neon', or 'Panhellenic Union of Fighting Youth'. PEAN was a rightist student group, based in Athens. It was not uncommon for siblings of PEAN members to belong to EPON, the EAM youth group and vice versa. 'It just depended on which group the rest of your "parea" (friends) had joined', said one informant.

12. The few organizations dedicated to the cause of women's emancipation, such as the Union for Women's Education founded in 1872, consisted almost exclusively of upper-class Athenian women. Generally, women's organizations in the pre-war period were the apolitical, philanthropic formations of urban, educated women with virtually no influence in the periphery.

13. See, 'On More Responsibilities for Women', Athens, 4th century B.C., Plato, Republic 5, and 'Men and Women Should Be Treated Alike', Plato, Laws 6, in Lefkowitz and Fant, *Women's Life in Greece and Rome: A Source Book in Translation*, Duckworth Ltd., London, 1982, pp. 66–75.

14. Campbell, John K., 'Traditional Values and Continuities in Greek Society', in *Greece in the 1980s*, edited by Richard Clogg, MacMillan Press in association with the Centre for Contemporary Greek Studies, King's College, University of London, 1983, p. 201.

15. See Diamandouros, P. Nikiforos, 'Greek Political Culture in Transition: Historical Origins, Evolution, Current Trends', in Clogg, *Greece in the 1980s*, pp. 43–69 and Psomas, Andreas I., *The Nation, the State, and the International System: The Case of Modern Greece*, A. Psomas in association with the National Center for Social Research, Athens, 1978.

16. Quote from interview, Hart/member of S.O.E. liaison spy network, Athens, February 7, 1985.

17. Here, 'resistance activity' is broadly defined to include any sort of insubordination aimed at defying the rules of the occupation, for which either imprisonment or death would have been the inevitable cost of being found out. Such acts, officially prohibited by SS decree, included: owning or using a radio; participating in neighbourhood soup kitchens; breaking curfew for any reason; knitting socks or supplying any kind of food or shelter to victims of the occupation.

      Accurate statistics are very difficult to obtain, if not non-existent. Organizational membership statistics are generally not available. This claim is based on my own estimate, using several sources plus a process of reasoning. Out of a population of 6–7 million with about 3.5 million women, if the women in other organizations, the women who worked in neighbourhood soup kitchens, and those who took part in non-organized, more informal resistance are counted, then it doesn't seem unreasonable to assume that about 1/3 of Greek women engaged in acts of resistance.

18. 'The martyrdom and death of Lela Karayanni', *Athens News*, 10 September 1985, translated and reprinted from *Kathemerini*. 'Lela Karayanni, at the time 42 years old (in 1941 when the German army marched into Athens) decided to fight against the occupation forces. Her life, consisting up to that point of raising her seven children, running her home, and being involved in several charity programs, changed forever . . . During the first six weeks of the Nazi occupation, Lela Karayanni, helped by her older children and using her own money, organized and successfully facilitated the escape of over 150 Greek and allied army officers and soldiers . . . (Later), in 1943, Lela Karayanni was asked by the allied headquarters to prepare the ground for the planned invasion of the Balkans, then favoured by Churchill. All the messages were sent via a hidden radio transmitter . . . When the location of the station was discovered by the Germans, the records were found and Karayanni was the first of several patriots to be arrested . . . She was executed by firing squad, three years after the Germans came to Athens, together with another 74 Greeks.'

19. See *Women in the Resistance: Personal Accounts*, op. cit., pp. 51–68. Mass village executions were, for a time, fairly common in Greece. Particularly hard-hit were areas of Central Greece, Thessaly, Roumeli, Macedonia, the Peloponnese, and the island of Crete, although atrocities were by no means limited to those regions.

20. In central Athens, the most notorious Nazi torture chambers were the 'Hotel Chrystal' and the 'Merlin' building near Kolonaki square. Haidari Prison, located in a western suburb of Athens, was one of the largest and most brutal of the Nazi bastilles in Greece. Its Cell Block 15 (to dekapende) was the departure point for trucks carrying groups of prisoners to mass execution at the firing range at Kaissariani, including the famous '200' who were shot on May 1, 1944. Groups also left Haidari for the German work-camps. A large group which included many women left Haidari for Ravensbruck and

other sites in the spring of 1944. It was widely rumoured that 'once you go to Haidari, you never come out alive'.

The main sources of information about Haidari prison are in Greek. The best account is by Andonis Floutzis, who was in the unique position of being the prison physician while simultaneously under arrest for his ongoing resistance activities. He is currently a prolific historian of the resistance era. (*Haidari: Prison Fortress and Altar of the National Resistance*, Papazisi Publishers, Athens, 1976.) Dr. Floutzis' job was to attend to the needs of sick and tortured prisoners, and to 'repair them again after the authorities or the war had abused them, so that they could later return to fight or be executed or tortured again'. (Interview, Athens, 30 April, 1985.) Other sources about Haidari are: Th. Kornaros, *Haidari Prison, Personal Account*, Chronos Publishers, Athens, 1982, distributed by Kastanioti Publishers, and *Haidari*, by Alexandros Zisis, Athens, 1969.

21. C. M. Woodhouse, *Apple of Discord*, W. B. O'Neill limited edition, 1985, p. 146.

22. Vasilis Rotas was a poet, writer, theatre producer and translator (of Shakespearean plays into Greek, for example), one of Greece's most prominent intellectuals both before and after the war.

23. The Political Committee for National Liberation was formed by EAM in the mountains in spring 1944 as a provisional government for Free Greece and was headquartered in the village of Viniani in the mountains of Thessaly. Its purpose was 'to organize and direct the national struggle for liberation, to administer the regions already liberated and to ensure the people's sovereignty over the whole country'. (Tsoucalas, *The Greek Tragedy*, Penguin, 1969, p. 70.

24. Hart/Interview, 22 October, 1985.

25. *The Hidden War*, Ch. 4 Documentary, January, 1986.

26. Hart/Interview, 4 November, 1985.

27. Hart/Interview, 25 November, 1985.

28. Hart/Interview, 3 December, 1985.

29. Ibid.

30. Hart/Interview, 18 October, 1985.

31. Hart/interview, 7 November, 1985.

32. Marion Sarafis, in Greece as an archaeology student in the 1930s, tells of overhearing a man refer to teachers travelling on a train as 'adespota koritsia' (masterless girls), the same adjective used to refer to stray dogs.

33. Hart/Interview, 14 September, 1985.

34. Hart/Interview, 27 May, 1985.

35. Plato, 'On More Responsibilities for Women', in *Women's Life in Greece and Rome*, op. cit., p. 68.

36. Considerable evidence exists that the White Terror actually began much before the German retreat, as early as 1943, when gangs such as the PAOtzides, the Sourlides, Colonel Grivas' X-ites, and the Papayianakides in Crete, collaborated with the Nazis and received from them the arms necessary to terrorize members of EAM–ELAS. For a review of development and codification of what Tsoucalas has called 'the neutralization of the ghost of EAM' (C. Tsoucalas, 'The Ideological Impact of the Civil War', in John Iatrides, *Greece in the 1940s: A Nation in Crisis*, University Press of New England, Hanover and London, 1981) which began in the spring of 1943 under the Rallis government, see Andre Gerolymatos, 'The Security Battalions and the Civil War', *Journal of the Hellenic Diaspora*, Vol. XII, No. 1, Spring, 1985, pp. 17–27. In Greek, Iannis Douyatzis, *I Tagmatasfalites*, presents evidence from documents and archives about the operations of the Government Security Battalions on the island of Euboea. Also see Alivizatos,

Nicos C., 'The "Emergency Regime" and Civil Liberties, 1946–1949', in *Iatrides*, pp. 220–228.

37. The youngest political prisoner in the Averoff Women's Section was Nina Ekonomou, called 'Ninaki' or 'Little Nina' by the other prisoners. She was 12½ years old when she arrived at the Averoff after being court-martialled in March of 1948, along with a 14 year old class-mate, Theofano Z. The girls claimed to have distributed anti-Nazi leaflets along with fellow EPON members from 'the best families and (some of whom were) the best students at our school'. Nina's mother was a high school teacher at Athens College. For an account of her trial, see (in Greek) Olympia Papadouka, *The Averoff Women's Prison*, Athens, 1981, pp. 68–70. Nina's prison class-mates, Georgia Poliyennous and the 16 year old Maria Repa, were executed on March 9, 1949.

38. According to the League for Democracy in Greece archives at King's College in London, a document called 'Biographies of the Eight Greek Women Political Prisoners' reveals that there were still former EAM women in the Averoff as late as February of 1965. A few sample descriptions are: *Prisoner A*: '48 years old. Took part, while very young, in the anti-fascist movement. During the occupation she fought the Nazis, was arrested in 1955, tortured by the security police, and after being detained for 5 years without trial was condemned to life imprisonment. Her only son is a refugee in Eastern Europe. Since the death of her mother, who fought with her in the mountains, Prisoner A has no close relatives left to care for her.' *Prisoner B:* '42 years old. With her only brother, who was killed during the struggle, Prisoner B participated in the fight against the Nazis. She was arrested in 1957 and condemned to life imprisonment. Her only relative is an aged sick mother.' *Prisoner C:* '65 years old. Comes from a Macedonian village. Her children are in Eastern Europe. She learned to read and write in prison. She was sent to prison because a radio transmitter was planted on her by the Gendarmes and she was unable to extricate herself from the trap. She is very sick and exhausted.' *Prisoner D:* '40 years old. Daughter of a veteran leader of the tobacco workers of Northern Greece who died in 1928 leaving four orphan children, who grew up in conditions of great hardship. Prisoner D was only 16 when the Nazis occupied Greece, but she joined the resistance and fought in its army, taking part in several battles against the Nazis, and in one of these her brother was killed at her side. She was persecuted in post-war Greece and in 1954 was arrested and tortured by the security police. Two years later she was framed on the basis of law 375 and sentenced to death (later commuted to life imprisonment) by a special court-martial in Athens. Is now in her eleventh year of imprisonment and her health is very poor.'

39. Hart/Interview, 25 November, 1985.

40. Tsoucalas, *The Greek Tragedy*, op. cit., p. 115.

41. The Dowry (Prika) system was very important in Greece, and in fact was only recently officially eradicated as part of the Family Law (1983). A girl without a dowry was handicapped in the marriage market. In fact, one of the activities of charitable women's organizations was to provide dowries for poor girls whose dowry property was destroyed during the war. Most of these efforts were not aimed at girls who had been in EAM, however. For the importance of the dowry and its post-war evolution, see Peter Allen, 'Internal Migration and the Changing Dowry in Modern Greece', *The Indiana Social Studies Quarterly*, Spring, 1979, pp. 142–156 and Juliet DuBoulay, 'The Meaning of Dowry: Changing Values in Rural Greece', *The Journal of Modern Greek Studies*, issue: Women and Men in Greece: A Society in Transition, May 1983, Johns Hopkins University Press.

119

42. *Ta Tragoudia Tis Antistasis Kai Tou Emfiliou*, (Songs of the Resistance and Civil War), Ellinika Themata, Athens, 1975.

43. I am grateful to Marion Sarafis for providing the information found in the previous 3 paragraphs.

44. Kraditor, Aileen S., *The Ideas of the Woman Suffrage Movement, 1890-1920*, W. W. Norton, 1981, p. 263.

45. *The Second Sex*, first published in France, 1949. First English translation, 1951.

46. See Mary Wollstonecraft, *A Vindication of the Rights of Woman*, 1792 and John Charvet, *Feminism*, J. M. Dent and Sons Ltd., London, 1982, especially Ch. 1.

47. See David Bouchier, *The Feminist Challenge: The Movements for Women's Liberation in Britain and the United States*, MacMillan Press, London, 1983, p. 43. Bouchier also quotes Friedan on McCall's magazine circa 1960, read by 5 million American women:

> 'The image of woman that emerges from this big, pretty magazine is young and frivolous, almost childlike; fluffy and feminine; passive, gaily content in a world of bedroom and kitchen, sex, babies and home. The magazine surely does not leave out sex; the only goal a woman is permitted is the pursuit of a man. It is crammed full of food, clothing, cosmetics, furniture and the physical bodies of young women, but where is the world of thought and ideas, the life of the mind and spirit?' (Friedan, Penguin, 1975, p. 32.)

48. Instead, see Eleni Stamiris, 'The Greek Women's Movement', *The New Left Review*, August, 1986 for a more comprehensive overview.

49. Hart/Interview, 4 November, 1985.

50. For example, a photograph from the League for Democracy in Greece archives at King's College shows broken glass, splintered wood, a typewriter in pieces, paper torn and scattered on the floor, and signs demolished. The caption reads, 'Women's Centre at Karditsa, wrecked April, 1945.

One of the delegates to the First Panhellenic Women's Conference stood up and began her speech with the following: 'I would like to direct the attention of our delegates to the following question which I consider to be extremely serious and to invite this body to take a formal stand on the matter. We all know that our country is, from every angle, experiencing difficult times and our people are suffering a lot. Naturally, our purpose here is not to lay blame or to make accusations of responsibility. But I would like to say this. The difficult lives of our people have taken an even more dramatic turn as a result of the killings and murders that are happening among us for political reasons. With each passing day, these take on more horrific proportions and are threatening to turn into a bonafide civil war if something is not done' (p. 154).

The delegates from Kalamata in the Peloponnese implored: 'We are witnesses to the fact that, even though we sacrificed our children, our men, our brothers and sisters (adelfia), our homes and our lives for the freedom and independence of our country, we have been overlooked by the "legal and social life" (sic) of our country and we are not allowed to express our opinions or to contribute to the reconstruction of our country. Besides that, we have been subjected to the most incredible persecutions, humiliations, tortures. They kill us, they rape us, they shave our heads, they publicly ridicule us. Our lives have become a constant trial' (p. 152).

51. (In Greek), documented from the archives of Rosa Imvrioti, Conference Secretary, *A' Panelladiko Synedrio Gynaikon – Athina, Mais 1946*, (First National Women's Conference), proceedings published by the Greek

Women's Federation (OGE), Athens, 1985.

52. Although the authors don't share my view of the resistance as *the* most important vehicle for social change in 20th century Greece, for an overview of women's changing social and legal status in the contemporary period, see Alice Yotopoulos-Marangopoulos, 'Some aspects of the legal status of women in Greece', and Zafiris Tzannatos, 'Comment on women's legal status and changing position in Greece', in *Socialism in Greece*, edited by Zafiris Tzannatos, Gower Press, 1986. In Greek, see Roula Kaklamanaki, *I Thesi Tis Ellinidas* (The Status of Greek Women), Kastanioti Publishers, 1984.

CONTEMPORARY GREEK HISTORY FOR ENGLISH READERS: AN ATTEMPT AT A CRITICAL ANALYSIS

Marion Sarafis

This essay arises from a need felt by the writer who has increasingly been asked to recommend reading-lists. Broadly speaking, the requests come in two categories: from specialists in other fields whose work has taken on a Greek dimension which calls for background briefing; and from visitors to Greece, attracted and interested beyond the resources of the guidebook, who sense a troubled history and want to know more. A further impetus has come from the somewhat intemperate reactions to the interpretation presented in Jane Gabriel's 3-part television series, *Greece: The Hidden War.*[1] These reactions will hardly have astonished Greeks but in the English-speaking world they may need explanation.

All history is interpretative and, to that extent, subjective.[2] A truly objective history is conceivable only as the mass of dated events, archival documents, statistics and memoirs which form the historian's raw material. In practice this is accessible only to specialist researchers. From it the historian, selects, interprets and concludes in accordance with his own viewpoint and this is true even of Ancient History, though the conscientious historian will interact with his material and, in turn, be influenced by what he finds. He should, of course, also draw attention to opposing interpretations where they exist. He acts as prism or filter.

Therefore, like economics and the other social sciences, history cannot but express a political position. At the receiving end too it is highly political. How a people or a nation sees itself and hence what political decisions it will take depends on how it sees its own history. One need cite

123

only three examples. That there is still amongst us a generation
(the writer's own) which grew up with the concept of the
British Empire does much to explain our present *malaise*
and obvious difficulty in finding an identity and a role.
Earlier, one might see in the dismemberment of the Habsburg
Empire at least a partial explanation for Austria's embrace of
Hitler and the Anschluss; and modern African historians can
tell us much of the effects of 'colonial history' on their
people.

All this may seem obvious but it must be stated because it
is highly relevant to recent Greek history and historiography.
The Liberation War of 1821–32 did not produce a truly
independent Greece but, as Byron had foretold, 'a colony of
the sovereigns of Europe',[3] with the result that in 1841 the
British Minister in Athens could say: 'A really independent
Greece is an absurdity. Greece is either Russian or English
and, since she must *not* be Russian, she must be English. . .'[4]
A pawn in Great Power struggles for Mediterranean and
Balkan influence, it is little wonder that Greece has had
difficulty in coming to terms with her own modern history
which did not take firm root as an academic discipline till
1975, whilst history subsequent to the First World War was
not even taught in schools. Though there had been
distinguished individual historians, a vacuum existed which,
on the one hand the 'protecting powers' (notably Britain and
after March 1947 the US) could fill with their own
exculpatory versions and, through client governments,
impose these on the Greek people; whilst, on the other,
Greek political parties could exploit this vacuum and the
passionate Greek interest in their history, for propaganda
purposes.

The aim must therefore be both to illustrate recent
advances in Greek contemporary historiography and to bring
into some kind of critical order the most accessible publications available to the English reader. For the latter purpose,
published translations from foreign languages will be included
whilst foreign language material in general will not. It must
be borne in mind that this excludes the very large corpus of
work – much of it by protagonists – available only in Greek.

In general, any student of recent Greek history will need
some knowledge of the remoter background without which
later events cannot be fully understood. This is more necessary

because of the highly individual Greek attitude to time-span, paralleled perhaps only in Ireland and possibly in Poland; in other words in countries with a long history of alien domination.

For Greeks their past and even their ancient and mythological past lives and breathes. Anyone who has heard Greek peasants at Epidaurus discussing the philosophical implications of the ancient dramas they have witnessed from the rocks above the amphitheatre will know what is meant. The Fall of Constantinople (1452) is, as Heinz Richter rightly says[5] the recent past, the nearly four centuries of Turkish rule the day before yesterday, the War of Independence (1821–32) yesterday and everything since then, at least since the First World War, is very presently to-day.

For this essay contemporary Greek history will be held to cover the years since 1936 and detailed English writing for an earlier period will not be included. But for the reasons just stated it is necessary to start with the general accounts and 'short histories' which will give the required background.

No better account could be found of Modern Greek History in its Balkan framework than Professor L. S. Stavrianos' monumental *The Balkans since 1453*. For purely Greek history, two earlier works: E. S. Forster's *A Short History of Modern Greece 1821–1956* and Bickham Sweet-Escott's *Greece: A Political and Economic Survey 1939–1953* still have their uses, but the two most up-to-date short histories available to-day are: Richard Clogg's *A Short History of Modern Greece* (from the start of the Byzantine downfall in 1204) and C. M. Woodhouse's *Modern Greece: A Short History* (starting from the founding of the Eastern Roman Empire in 324 AD). Both have recently been re-issued, up-dated to 1985. Richard Clogg is an academic historian and C. M. Woodhouse, as head of the British (later Allied) Military Mission to the wartime Greek Resistance, was a protagonist in some of the events he recounts. The writer has greater experience of using Clogg and has found his concise presentation of complicated developments a useful model. Both are factually reliable reference histories but neither, in the writer's opinion, will give the reader an insight into that history as seen by Greeks themselves.

Fortunately there is a book which (albeit out of print) can supply the need for a Greek voice: Constantine Tsoucalas'

The Greek Tragedy, published in 1969. This is a narrative rather than a reference history and can be faulted on the occasional point of detail but it presents a viewpoint in the mainstream Republican tradition which would probably be shared by most Greeks not firmly committed to the Right.

On particular aspects of Modern Greek History, Nicos Mouzelis' *Modern Greece: Facets of Underdevelopment* is essential for social and economic history. For political history we have so far had Carey and Carey's *The Web of Modern Greek Politics*, to which we can now add an essential reference work, Richard Clogg's *Parties and Elections in Greece: The Search for Legitimacy*, which gives a complete conspectus of post-war elections and plebiscites, with statistical analysis and a history of the political parties. Thanos Veremis' *Greek Security Considerations: A Historical Perspective* analyses Greek foreign and defence policy over the last 150 years; whilst, because Greece's strategic position has given foreign influence an undue role in her history, it may be worth pointing to a specific study of this subject: *Foreign Interference in Greek Politics* by T. A. Couloumbis *et al.* A more personal and literary account of 20th century events can be found in Compton Mackenzie's *Greece in my life*, best described as a summary of his more extended *AEgean Memories, First Athenian Memories, Gallipoli Memories, Greek Memoirs.*

A 19th century problem which has become topical since 1983 is presented in a well-researched book *The Elgin Marbles: Should they be returned to Greece?* by Christopher Hitchens, a firm but fair advocate of return.

Finally, the reader should be aware of a good bibliography. Heinz Richter's *Greece and Cyprus since 1920: Bibliography of Contemporary History* (11,500 titles) should be available in all academic and the better public libraries.

The Metaxas Dictatorship 1936–1941

I have chosen to start the more detailed analysis with this period because, for Greeks, it forms a continuum with the events of the Second World War. This was stressed at the first Greek International Historians' Conference, organised in Athens in 1984 by a committee based on the University of Crete, which made 1936–44 its terms of reference.[6] In fact, an understanding of what happened in wartime Greece is impossible without some insight into the Metaxas dictatorship and, in particular, into the monarch's responsibility for this, for which reason Greeks speak of 'monarcho-fascism'. This made the constitutional issue the overriding problem of Greece's post-war future and, in turn, raises the whole problem of British policy which, in its barely-concealed support of its royal protégé's preference for unconstitutional rule through a fascist-inclined dictator, faithfully mirrored the appeasement policies of the period; whilst anticipating to-day's US preference for authoritarian despots in client states. For this reason the subject is a painful one for British historians to treat, though Clogg is somewhat more critical of Metaxas than Woodhouse.

Again, we must turn to Greeks or Greek-Americans writing in English. The best short account is probably that in Professor L. S. Stavrianos' *Greece: American Dilemma and Opportunity* and, should this prove hard to find to-day, there is Tsoucalas and the relevant chapter of John Louis Hondros' *Occupation and Resistance: The Greek Agony 1941-1944*. Fuller accounts can be found in Jon V. Kofas' *Authoritarianism in Greece* (with a good bibliography) and in John S. Koliopoulos' *Greece and the British Connection 1935-1941* which deals specifically with British policy fluctuations.

Assessment of Metaxas has been bedevilled by his celebrated 'NO' to the Italian invasion of 1940 and here the writer finds Koliopoulos somewhat lenient. Metaxas could do no other than he did since he was caught in a pincers' movement between King and people, for once united — though for wholly different reasons — in their will to resist. Since he had no popular base but depended on the King (who in turn depended on the British), it was a question of his political survival.

For the atmosphere of the Metaxas dictatorship and its two major crimes: institutionalisation of torture (responsible for much later violence) and the attempt to create a popular base through a compulsory Hitlerjugend-style Youth Movement, one must turn to two books which are not strictly historical. *Exiles in the Aegean* by the Australian journalist, Bert Birtles, 1938, would be worth finding for its account of how the regime treated its active opponents; whilst a child's-eye view of the Youth Movement comes through vividly in what is perhaps the only Greek children's book to have achieved an English edition, *Wildcat under glass* by Alki Zeï, most probably autobiographical.

Finally, from the Metaxas period right through to 1947, an illuminating running commentary will be found in the published reports of the US ambassador of the time: *Ambassador MacVeagh Reports: Greece 1933–1947.*

On a personal note, it was a first acquaintance with Greece as a post-graduate archaeological student during the Metaxas period and the problems it raised in regard to British involvement which altered the subsequent course of the writer's life.

The Axis Invasion 1940–1941

With the exception of Kofas, whose account ends in 1939, all the books recommended above cover the Axis invasion since they take their accounts up at least to the dictator's death in January 1941. Protagonists speak in Churchill's *The Second World War*, Vol. III and in General Alexandros Papagos' *The Battle of Greece 1940–1941.* For the German invasion *Greek Tragedy '41* by A. Heckstall-Smith and H. T. Baillie-Grohman and *Greece and Crete 1941* can be recommended and there is an attractive personal memoir of the Cretan campaign by Theodore Stephanides, *Climax in Crete.* Compton Mackenzie's *The Wind of Freedom* complements these factual histories. Sidelights from an unorthodox angle may be found in Sarafis' *ELAS: Greek Resistance Army.*[7]

Occupation and Resistance 1941–1944

To a French or German reader, in each case, two books could be recommended which would solve their problem.[8] For the English reader, confronted with a potentially confusing plethora of published material, due to British involvement and to the controversial character of British policy, there may be need of critical assessment and definition of category and standpoint. But there is one fact which must never be lost from view: there is an equal plethora of authoritative Greek writing inaccessible to all but readers of Modern Greek. Of the top-level protagonists, Hajis, Ioannidis, Papandreou, Partsalidis, Pyromaglou, Rousos, Sarafis and

Vafiadis have all written memoirs (Hajis, Rousos and Vafiadis at multi-volume length). Of these only Sarafis and a selection of Papandreou's articles are accessible in English and Sarafis' account is a memoir of his own experiences rather than a comprehensive history of the Resistance. This is to make no mention of the grass-roots memoirs and the work of Greek historians.

Therefore, so as not to lose sight of the Greek perspective, the books by Greek–American historians, Professor Stavrianos and Dr. Hondros, and of course Tsoucalas' *Greek Tragedy*, should be used as a mirror for the assessment of British sources.

Four books, three by top-level protagonists and one an academic history, seem to the writer the minimum required reading for an appreciation of wartime Greek history.

The recognised British, or should one call it 'Chatham House' viewpoint is best presented by C. M. Woodhouse in his *Apple of Discord*, recently re-issued. Here, in the form of a detailed account of his experiences with the British and later Allied Military Mission to the Greek Resistance, which he led from summer 1943, he gives what will probably remain the classic presentation of the British case.

For the Greek left-wing Resistance viewpoint, at least an equal weight should be given to General Sarafis' *ELAS: Greek Resistance Army*, recounting his own direct experiences as ELAS C-in-C. This was written immediately after the events it relates but I can say with pleasure that, unlike many memoirs of protagonists, the passage of time has served it well since much that the author advanced as only tentative hypothesis has been confirmed since British official documents became available in the '70s.

Brigadier E. C. W. Myers' *Greek Entanglement* owes its importance mainly to his position as first head of the British Military Mission and to his authoritative account of the Gorgopotamos operation of November 1942. But the recent re-issue brings us something more which gives the book its place in the 'required reading' section. This is the Appendix in which he now tells us of his disagreement with Churchill and the Foreign Office over the Greek constitutional problem and the need to re-assure Greeks that the King would not return without a referendum. The writer has little doubt that, had his advice been heeded, most of what happened later in

Greece could have been avoided. Instead, he suffered the fate inevitable for those who give sound but unwelcome advice – he was removed from Greece and his career was blocked.

For the academic history of British wartime policy, we must again go to a Greek, writing in English on the basis of British official documents. Procopis Papastratis' *British Policy towards Greece during the Second World War 1941–1944* gives the documentary background to the protagonists' memoirs. No reader need fear that this will be heavy-going. Dr. Papastratis writes with an enviable stylistic grace and a gentle irony which gave more than one occasion for quiet laughter. What he does prove beyond doubt is the concentration of British policy on restoring the monarchy and its advocates' inability to comprehend why their efforts to 'sell' the King to the Greeks met with such determined sales-resistance. Here the Foreign Office paid the price (or rather the Greeks were to pay it) of a trait noted elsewhere by C. M. Woodhouse[9] – their failure to attach any importance to Greek popular opinion. Dr. Papastratis concludes that the policy would have been the same had no left-wing Resistance existed. As Sarafis said of Churchill, 'He acted in the interests of the British Empire, as he saw them'. The trouble was that there would be no place for this concept in the post-war world.

By way of a documentary footnote to these four major books, a selection of British reports from wartime Greece has been edited by Dr. Lars Baerentzen under the title *British Reports on Greece 1943–1944*. Dr. Baerentzen had the ingenious idea of annotating these reports with the variant versions of events recorded in Sarafis' *ELAS*.

The attitude of other Allied Powers and of neighbours to events in Greece is perhaps worth separate mention. For the Soviet attitude, a remarkable paper by the late Elisabeth Barker; 'Greece in the framework of Anglo-Soviet Relations 1941–1947' can be found in *Greece: From Resistance to Civil War*. For the US the subject is treated in L. S. Wittner's *American Intervention in Greece 1943–1949* (of which more later). Just why the British so distrusted the American OSS agents in Greece finds lively illustration in Costas Couvaras' diary: *O.S.S. with the Central Committee of EAM*. Like Couvaras, they were mostly Americans of Greek origin and, in the final resort, they judged and felt as Greeks. Yugoslav criticism of the Greek left-wing Resistance finds expression in a rare document, now re-issued, Svetozar Vukmanović (General Tempo) on *How and Why the People's Liberation Army of Greece met with defeat.*

Two further books from Greek–American authors deserve mention here: John Louis Hondros' *Occupation and Resistance: The Greek Agony 1941–1944* because it is the only account in English where use has been made of German archival sources; and Eleni Fourtouni's *Greek Women in Resistance* because this is a topic normally overlooked.

Other special themes are the wartime famine, described at the time by S. L. Hourmouzios in his *Starvation in Greece* and the 'mutinies' in the Greek Middle East forces for which recourse must be had to journals: L. S. Stavrianos on 'The Mutiny in the Greek Armed Forces, April 1944'; and Hagen Fleischer, 'The Anomalies in the Greek Middle East Forces 1941–1944'.

There remain three other categories which, because they are easily available to the English reader, perhaps need summary comment.

In one case this will be a word of warning. Greek Resistance history is too complicated to be satisfactorily treated in generalised accounts of European resistance movements. The same no doubt holds good for all the national movements but the writer is only competent to speak for Greece. The general tendency is towards uncritical acceptance of the 'Chatham House' version, to say the least, and this is even true of the established Second World War historian, M. R. D. Foot. An honourable exception must however be made for David Stafford's *Britain and European Resistance 1941–1945*. The Greek section shows evidence of independent research and, for this writer, has made a useful contribution by confirming from British records what she had previously only suspected.

The second category, published conference proceedings, tends to be known only to the specialist but these often contain nuggets of invaluable information. So one must list the three main publications covering this period: *British Policy towards Wartime Resistance in Yugoslavia and Greece*, edited by Phyllis Auty and Richard Clogg: *Greece in the 1940s: A Nation in Crisis*, edited by John O. Iatrides; and *Greece: From Resistance to Civil War* edited by M. Sarafis (reference to particular papers has been made where appropriate).

Lastly, we have the memoirs of British Liaison Officers and other participants, a corpus so extensive that the writer must doubt whether she has fully caught up with it, more especially with what may have been published elsewhere in the English-speaking world. The memoirs of Nigel Clive, Nicholas Hammond, Denys Hamson, William Jordan, W. Stanley Moss and John Mulgan are listed in the bibliography, whilst Lt.-Col. Arthur Edmunds' memoirs remain unpublished in New Zealand. Because it is something slightly different, mention must be made of *Kiriakos* by Don Turner, the story of a private soldier, Ernest Chapman, an escaped prisoner of the invading Germans, who spent his war fighting with Greek guerrilla groups, mainly with ELAS. Whilst it must be remembered that this is Chapman's story as told to a freelance journalist, the difference in approach from that of most BLO memoirs is interesting. Where the BLOs in general do not question British policy, this son of the Yorkshire mines, though he did not go all the way with the more revolutionary objectives of some of his comrades-in-arms, nevertheless, when he eventually rejoined the BLOs, did not hesistate to tell them that he thought British policy was impeding support to those who were really fighting the common enemy. It must also be borne in mind, when considering the BLO memoirs, that the only officer to come out positively in support of EAM–ELAS, Lt.-Col. Rufus Sheppard (Hills), was killed under controversial circumstances during the December 1944 fighting and therefore left no testimony.

To these narratives must be added two by Greeks who served with the BLOs: Chris Jecchinis' *Beyond Olympus* and George Psychoundakis' *The Cretan Runner*. Finally, C. M. Woodhouse's autobiographical *Something Ventured* adds an interesting personal supplement to his *Apple of Discord*. To summarise, it may be said that this category of reading matter varies in quality from the useful contributory source to the simple adventure story.

The Events of December 1944

That Britain should find herself in armed conflict with the main Greek wartime Resistance Movement, EAM–ELAS, came as a surprise and shock to British public opinion and, not least, to most of the British troops brought in at liberation, whose reception had certainly not prepared them for this. Now of course, reading Myers, Sarafis and Woodhouse and with Dr. Papastratis' documented study, we can see its inevitability. But we still need the authors who show what paved the way for violence and the books which analyse the circumstances of the clash.

To start with the protagonists: Sarafis' *ELAS* and Woodhouse's *Apple of Discord* maintain their primacy and to these must be added, from the British standpoint, Vol. VI of Churchill's *The Second World War* and Ambassador Leeper's memoir *When Greek meets Greek*, which contains at least one useful admission of early consideration of the use of force. From the EAM–ELAS angle it is unfortunate that the English edition of the *EAM White Book* is unlikely to be available, even in university libraries. Stavrianos remains a reliable guide and later academic analysis is provided by John Iatrides' *Revolt in Athens* which sees the December events as a 'cumulation of error'.

But an assessment depends on the answer to certain questions of detail. Here a valuable paper by George Alexander: 'The Demobilization crisis of November 1944' in *Greece in the 1940s* shows how Prime Minister George Papandreou's deliberate mis-representation of an agreement for demobilisation of all Greek armed units brought about the resignation of the EAM ministers from the Government of National Unity. An unarmed EAM protest demonstration was fired on by Greek Government police (eye-witness account by W. Byford-Jones in *The Greek Trilogy* and a fuller account by Lars Baerentzen in *Scandinavian Studies in Modern Greek*, No. 2, 1978). It was this and firing again the next day at the funeral of the victims which sparked the clash between EAM–ELAS and the Greek Government in which the British gave armed support to the latter.

In general, Byford-Jones' memoir is a useful account of the December period and its aftermath and should be supplemented by an eloquent voice from the ranks. Colin Wright's *British Soldier in Greece*. Public Relations-style statements of the British case, such as the journalist, Richard Capell's highly prejudiced *Simiomata* and Henry Maule's later *Scobie: Hero of Greece* are probably less helpful. On the other hand,

Hugh Williamson's history of *The Fourth Division* based on War Office documents and sanctioned by the army authorities, makes it clear that the army did not hold with the theory of an attempt by EAM and KKE to seize power.

But the liberation and December period has left some curious unanswered questions. Evan Sarafis himself could only guess at EAM's reasons for not letting him bring the trained mountain ELAS to the support of the irregular 'urban guerrillas' fighting in Athens and it is hard to resist the conclusion that EAM did not want a full-scale confrontation but merely hoped to bring down the Papandreou Government with which they could no longer co-operate. Another area awaiting elucidation is the curious tacit agreement between British and Germans for a peaceful German withdrawal without surrender of their arms to ELAS, an understanding which, in Crete, developed into a kind of condominium. This has been adumbrated by Hondros, examined by Lars Baerentzen and will be the subject of a forthcoming article by Heinz Richter.[10]

Since what is under question here is the basic policy of EAM and KKE (The Greek Communist Party), treated in Vol. II of this book by Pericles Grambas, this may be the place to mention the various studies of KKE. It must be said with regret that the best studies of this subject to date are in French, German and Italian (with a Greek edition).[11] John C. Loulis' *The Greek Communist Party 1940–1944* and D. George Kousoulas' *Revolution and Defeat: The story of the Greek Communist Party* (of which more in the Civil War section) both have a strong odour of the 'Cold War tract' and the former can be – and has been – taken apart on points of factual accuracy.[12] However, an important paper by Haris Vlavianos entitled 'The Greek Communist Party in search of revolution' appeared in April 1989 in Messrs Routledge's series *Resistance and Revolution in Mediterranean Europe.* This is now the best recommendation for English readers.

From Liberation to Civil War: The British 'Protectorate' 1945–1947

It is at this point that the main protagonists leave us. Sarafis had planned a sequel to *ELAS* but, at his death in 1957, had only completed a rough draft of the first chapter.[13]

Woodhouse becomes an observer rather than a leading participant. Until the appearance of the recently-published academic studies, we had to make do with a patchwork of sources.

From participants we have Harold Macmillan's account of the negotiations following the armistice between the Greek Government and ELAS in Vol. II of *The Blast of War* and we have the already-cited memoirs and reports of Ambassadors Leeper and MacVeagh. A useful 'handbook' to the period is *The Greek Dilemma* by the then US military attaché in Athens, William Hardy McNeill, which rates high on accuracy and objective reporting. From British observers holding official posts we have Geoffrey Chandler's *A Divided Land*; whilst Nigel Clive's *A Greek Experience* covers this period more sketchily than the wartime years (perhaps on account of his Embassy position). For the Greek angle we must still look to Tsoucalas and above all to Stavrianos.

Two books which appeared in the early '70s probably attained wider circulation than any of these and can perhaps best be termed 'popular histories'. C. M. Woodhouse's *The Struggle for Greece 1941–1949* is an attempt to look at the whole period: Resistance, interim and Civil War. But, though it is useful in testifying to the role of right-wing terrorist backlash in creating the conditions for civil war, it nowhere attains the weight and depth of *Apple of Discord*.

The second book bears even more clearly the hallmark of popular history. This is *The Kapitanios*,[14] translated from the French of Dominique Eudes. Here again there is an attempt to cover the whole period from Resistance to Civil War. The appearance of this book was welcome at the time because, between the two editions of Sarafis *ELAS* (abridged 1951; definitive 1980) and with Stavrianos not easily accessible outside the US, here at last was a voice for the Greek Left. The lively writing, in film-scenario style, and the build-up of the problematic and tragic personality of Aris Velouchiotis into a kind of Greek Che Guevara combined to ensure an appeal to the young. But it is not strong on accuracy and seems to hover uneasily between popular history and *roman à thèse*. One cannot but feel that informants were chosen and facts selected in order to sustain a previously-determined hypothesis. Some of this was tidied up in the English edition which may therefore be preferable to the original French.

With official archives for the period becoming accessible here and in the US during the '70s, the '80s have brought us two academic histories which, since they sustain widely-differing interpretations would seem to bear out the writer's introductory remarks on historiography. George Alexander's *The Prelude to the Truman Doctrine: British Policy in Greece 1944-1947* presents a broadly supportive account of British policy with which proponents of the 'Chatham House' version will have no quarrel. Within its limits it is well-researched and, since the author is a Greek–American, the more obvious Greek sources have been consulted.

A much fuller and more critical account, even more deeply-researched, especially in the field of Greek sources, is Heinz Richter's *British Intervention in Greece: From Varkiza to Civil War*.[15] Dr. Richter highlights not only Woodhouse's revealing Peloponnese report (unmentioned by its author) but also Churchill's embarrassing preference for Greek collaborators rather than left-wing resisters and the constant use in Foreign Office documents of 'protectorate' analogies and terminology, matters for which we could look in vain to Alexander, though we must not forget his services in revealing the misdeeds of George Papandreou in November 1944 (see p. 133). What Dr. Richter does demonstrate is how easily the 1945 Labour Government could have reversed Churchill's Greek policy at a time when Greece was penetrated and controlled by British Missions.

The conclusion most likely to force itself upon the reader from these studies is that the Greek civil war of 1947–9 was the almost inevitable result of the White Terror which followed the events of December 1944 and literally forced the resistance men back into the mountains for their own safety; and that Britain, in her role as protecting power, making and unmaking prime ministers, bore a large measure of responsibility for this state of affairs.

The Civil War 1947–1949

Thus the Civil War should not, in the writer's opinion, be seen as a continuation of wartime left-wing resistance, but as an entirely different matter, an almost desperate reaction to conditions of terrorism prevailing everywhere outside Athens. This is perhaps the place to state that she does not accept the theory of the 'three rounds' in a Greek Communist attempt to seize power. This seems to her altogether too facile and, unfortunately, too verbally convenient a descriptive short-cut. All three outbreaks of internecine strife were different in origin and context. The fighting between EAM–ELAS and EDES in 1943–4 was a territorial squabble between armed groups caused by encroachments on previously-agreed boundaries, no doubt encouraged by the British in the case of EDES. The second in December 1944 started as a deliberately low-key reaction by the political organisations aimed at producing a change in the Government of National Unity and therefore the mountain ELAS — for all its commanders' readiness — was not brought in. The third, the Civil War, was a reaction to terror compounded by tactical blunders on the part of KKE and particularly of its General-Secretary, Zachariadis, who had returned to Greece in 1945 from imprisonment in Dachau. Of these blunders quite the most disastrous was abstention in the elections of March 1946.[16] Support against the 'three rounds' inter-pretation can be found in Hondros, in Pericles Grambas' paper in Vol. II and in a recent remark by C. M. Woodhouse: 'I have no doubt at all that they (EAM–ELAS) could have occupied Athens at the time when the Germans left and they could have made it difficult for allied forces to return to Greece without having to face an opposed landing.'[17] If EAM and KKE could have done this, then the fact that they did not can only mean that the intention was lacking.

After this explanatory parenthesis it must be said that academic work on the Civil War is still in progress. The first conferences have been held and one volume of Conference Proceedings has already appeared.[18] There exists as yet no standard general work to which the reader can be confidently referred, though readers of French would be well-served meanwhile with Christophe Chiclet's book (referred to in footnote 8). At a more general level there are Eudes and Woodhouse.

Richter's *British Intervention in Greece* gives a good account of the run-up and the best brief general account is perhaps the paper on 'Civil War 1945–1949' contributed by Professor Iatrides to *Greece in the 1940s*. There are two studies from an expressly Right-wing viewpoint: Edgar

O'Ballance's *The Greek Civil War 1944–1949* which seems to be one in a series of studies of 'insurgencies' by the same author. The other (already mentioned) is by a 'repentant' Greek Communist, D. George Kousoulas' *Revolution and Defeat: The story of the Greek Communist Party*. The author, who now teaches in the US was later an active supporter of the Colonels' Junta, involved in preparing their so-called Constitution. More need hardly be said. Research failures can be found in both books.

Two personal memoirs are valuable for their well-written stories of experiences in Greece during the Civil War. One is Kenneth Matthews' *Memories of a Mountain War*. He was the BBC correspondent who found himself kidnapped by the Democratic Army and suffered later for the exceedingly fair account he gave of this experience. The other is Kevin Andrews' *The Flight of Ikaros*, recently re-issued in a revised edition. This account of a traveller's conversations at grass-roots level is not only an early study in oral history but perhaps the best book to recommend to the intelligent tourist who wants to understand the burden of memory carried by the average elderly or middle-aged Greek. The only pity from the historian's viewpoint is that both books are set in the Peloponnese and that we have nothing comparable for the more important civil war areas in Northern Greece. Here one may mention a curiosity: Mihri Belli's *Rigasin Dediği: What Rigas said*. This is a memoir in Turkish, with an extended English summary, by the only non-Greek to fight with the Democratic Army — a Turk who was recruited from Istanbul to help and advise with the Turkish minority population in Thrace.

But the main problem of the Civil War period concerns the role of the US after the promulgation of the Truman Doctrine in March 1947, and for this we are better informed. Not only have we Professor Stavrianos' previously-mentioned book and a more general study of *Greek–American Relations* by Theodore Couloumbis and John Iatrides, but there is a splendid book based almost entirely on US official documents: Lawrence S. Wittner's *American Intervention in Greece 1943–1949*. It is difficult to underrate the importance of this book which does for US policy what Papastratis and Richter do for British policy. In addition it should be remembered that what the US did in Greece served as blueprint for subsequent actions in Vietnam, Grenada and Latin America.

It is to be hoped that, when the academic histories are written the appalling Makronisos concentration camp will not be forgotten. There is still time to tape-record the younger survivors but so far only the women's experience has reached us in Eleni Fourtouni's *Greek Women in Resistance*. There is no lack of published source material in Greek, as the experience is one with which Greeks have to come to terms in much the same way as Germans have to come to terms with Dachau (I expressly exclude the gas-chamber camps from the comparison). For this reason it has had some prominence as a theme for both literary and cinema work. An English effort of this type would seem to be Rex Warner's novel *Men of Stones*, a probable result of his experiences with the British Council in Athens at the time.

It remains only to attempt an assessment of what a historian friend has described as 'that somewhat conspicuously promoted book'. Nicholas Gage's *Eleni* which even achieved the cinematic accolade vainly aspired to by Eudes; though it should be noted in passing that a boycott by Greek cinema technicians and local opposition meant that the filming had to be transferred to Spain and the film was anyway a failure. This 470 pp. book is based on one fact which no one seeks to deny: that the author's mother, Eleni Gatzoyanni, was executed by the Democratic Army in the Epirus village of Lia in 1948. Perhaps the most balanced – and tactful – verdict is that of Professor Iatrides: '*Eleni* is a traumatic experience but it is not history.'[19] If Eudes sometimes suggests *roman à thèse, Eleni* can only be called *faction*. The bare facts and the village background (which has interest) could have been given in a third of the space and the 'historical' padding is highly tendentious. Executions are an unfortunate fact of civil war and Eleni was certainly involved in organising an escape party to reach Greek Government army lines. But no mention is made of the over 3,000 executions carried out by the Greek Government between 1946–50.[20] A bare statement of the facts would have commanded respect and sympathy; or the case could have been made the basis for a novel, like the excellent resistance and civil war novels of Stratis Haviaras, in which case the criteria would be different. As it is, the book offends against Greek susceptibilities by exploiting a mother's tragedy for the creation of a best-seller. As one English critic of the resulting film expressed it: 'the real Eleni did not deserve to be buried a second time under lies.'[21]

By way of postscript, a rumour has reached the writer which she would prefer not to believe: that this book is being recommended to students for their reading-lists. This would be justifiable only if the object was to teach them to discriminate and to recognise what is *not* history. Are the same students being directed to Professor Wittner's valuable book?

The 'false dawn' of normality 1950–1967. The Cyprus problem

For this long and complex period we must rely mainly on Tsoucalas, with Clogg's *Parties and Elections in Greece: The Search for Legitimacy* as essential for sequence of political developments. A perhaps deeper analysis of this period by Jean Meynaud is available only in French and Greek.[22] Couloumbis' and Iatrides' *Greek–American Relations* will continue to illuminate its subject and to it we may now add Yiannis Roubatis' *Tangled Webs: The US in Greece 1947–1967*. The author was until recently a PASOK Government spokesman and he leaves the reader in little doubt of the sacrifices imposed on Greece in the name of US 'stability', to which the Junta *coup* provided a rather too obviously welcome solution. Nicholas Stavrou's *Allied Policy and Military Interventions: The political role of the Greek military*, like – at a narrative level – Part I of Philip Deane's *I should have died*, deal with US policy and CIA operations in the run-up to the Junta *coup*.

Two books are important because one is about and the other is by a protagonist and, as such, they represent the two competing forces which dominated Greek political life at this period. One is C. M. Woodhouse's *Karamanlis: The Restorer of Greek Democracy*. This is a ·biography of the former Greek Prime Minister and later President, written at his own request:[23] a curious book because, whilst the tone is one of uncritical encomium — almost hagiography — it nevertheless contains allusions (comprehensible only to the specialist) which come perilously close to 'taking the mickey'. Whilst the portrait which emerges cannot be uncritically accepted, the political history is useful. The other is the recent Greek Prime Minister, Andreas Papandreou's *Democracy at Gunpoint*. Here we have a top-level account from the opposite viewpoint of events leading up to the Junta and of the Junta period itself. A simultaneous reading of these two books might well be the best way to reach an understanding of the years when Greek life struggled so painfully towards normality, only to be frustrated in 1967. The voice of the Resistance Left is missing here. For 1952–7 the writer has tried to give some indication of the effort to re-organise in the third section of her biographical intro-duction to Sarafis' *ELAS*.[24]

But the main interest for the British reader in this period will probably be directed towards the Cyprus problem which became acute in the mid-fifties. Heinz Richter's paper in Vol. II will prove invaluable here and for how the problem was seen in Greece Woodhouse on Karamanlis and Andreas Papandreou are authoritative. The troubles of the mid-fifties, when Cyprus first offered active resistance to British rule produced two more or less immediate British studies: Percy Arnold's *Cyprus Challenge* and Charles Foley's *Island in Revolt*. Both books accepted the anachronistic character of British colonial rule and Foley's book caused something of a scandal at the time of its appearance in 1962. Foley later edited *The Memoirs of General Grivas*, the EOKA commander whom — as we have now learned from Mr. Gough Whitlam's testimony in the *Spycatcher* trial — MI6 was planning to assassinate. The attempted *coup* of 1974 and the Turkish invasion have since prompted two new Cyprus histories: *Cyprus* by Christopher Hitchens and the somewhat fuller *A New History of Cyprus* by Stavros Panteli.

The Colonels' Junta 1967–1974

The run-up to these seven years of darkness is covered by the books examined in the previous section. To summarise: Twelve years of government by the Right (1952–1964) had ended with the election of a Centre government under the premiership of George Papandreou and for the first time since the end of the civil war real progress had been made towards the restoration of human rights and freedom of expression. But Papandreou's attempts to bring the army to heel were frustrated by the young king Constantine who

provoked the premier's resignation in much the same constitutionally dubious way as his grandfather had provoked
that of the liberal statesman Venizelos, in 1915. A holding
government of apostates from Papandreou's Centre Union
was charged with preparing elections due in May 1967.

But it seemed that normalisation had gone too far for the
army (in January 1967 there remained only 11 political
prisoners) and it was widely expected that elections would
be immediately followed by a *coup* at high level, probably
by generals with covert Palace backing. But, on 21st April,
a group of colonels with Greek CIA and reportedly even
collaborationist pasts, got in first and established − with
what degree of US connivance has not yet become fully
clear − an authoritarian regime, characterised by suspension
of the Constitution and parliament, the re-opening of the
courts-martial and the concentration camps and the
institutionalisation of modern torture practices. In addition,
the remarkably low intellectual calibre of the main
protagonists contributed to make the regime not only hateful
but singularly ridiculous. The arch-dictator, Colonel
Papadopoulos, seemed incapable of coherent expression.[25]

This new crisis produced a spate of books on Greece. To
take the general treatments first: Tsoucalas remains essential
and so does Andreas Papandreou's *Democracy at Gunpoint*.
In England the Junta found only one serious if reserved
apologist, David Holden, whose *Greece without columns:
The Making of the Modern Greeks* seems based on the
premise that they deserved no better; there is also Taki
Theodoracopoulos' *The Greek Upheaval*, an individualistic
study, of occasional use to the specialist. In 1972 there
appeared a weighty and highly critical study: *Greece under
Military Rule*, edited by Richard Clogg and George Yannopoulos, with 12 papers by experts, mainly Greek, covering
most facets of the Junta regime. From the US we have *Greece
under the Junta* by Peter Schwab and George D. Frangos in
the Facts on File series, a chronological account useful for
reference purposes; also Stephen Rousseas' *The Death of
a Democracy*, a good brief account covering all essentials.
Greece in the Dark is a collection of powerful essays by
Kevin Andrews, author of the much-praised *Flight of Ikaros*,
the product of his life in Athens under the Junta. Finally,
we have C. M. Woodhouse's *The Rise and Fall of the Greek*

Colonels, a useful if not a definitive analysis, rather stronger on the Cyprus events which led to the Junta's downfall than on conditions within Greece itself.

Two specialised books deal with what were two of the most significant aspects of the Junta regime. James Becket's *Barbarism in Greece* is an American lawyer's enquiry into the use of torture (and in this context we should not forget Amnesty International's *Torture in Greece* based on reports of the First Torturers' Trial in 1975). The other is Robert McDonald's *Pillar and Tinderbox: The Greek Press and the Dictatorship* which includes a useful epilogue on the aftermath.

Like the wartime Resistance, the Junta experience produced several memoirs of personal experience, for the most part written during the later Junta years when their authors were political refugees and hence first published in English or French. Besides Andreas Papandreou's already-mentioned book, there is his wife Margaret's lively *Nightmare in Athens*. Two distinguished women whom readers may remember in London were the newspaper proprietor and editor, Helen Vlachos, who escaped from *House Arrest* (the title of her memoir) and Lady Amalia Fleming, Greek widow of the discoverer of penicillin, who was deported after a court-marial trial which ended with a prison sentence. Like Helen Vlachos' book, her *A Piece of Truth* deals with a single personal — but highly dramatic and revealing — experience. *The Method* by Perikles Korovessis is a personal account of torture, an illustration of the system analysed by James Becket. The composer, Mikis Theodorakis' *Journal of Resistance* tells the story of his active opposition to the Junta from its earliest days. For those who want to read a real-life detective story, Richard Cottrell's *Blood on their hands: The killing of Ann Chapman* puts a strong, though not yet a conclusive case for Junta Security Service responsibility for the killing of the young British journalist. A valuable account of the later Junta period from autumn 1969 is given by the Netherlands ambassador, Carl Barkman, *Ambassador in Athens*.

For the actual fall of the Junta in July 1974, Woodhouse's biography of Karamanlis and his *Rise and Fall of the Greek Colonels* and Hitchens' and Panteli's books on Cyprus cover the main events, though the final word on the exact extent of US involvement in the Cyprus disaster is still awaited.

The Present Day

With the fall of the Junta, Greece entered on a new and we may hope a happier period of her history. A referendum made the country a republic, freedom of expression was restored, the Communist Party was legalised and the demotic or popular language (see pp. 25–51) became official. Whether membership of the EEC, which Karamanlis had made the main plank of his post-Junta premiership, will really benefit Greece probably depends on the way that institution itself develops but, at least, membership makes further *coups* less likely and gives Greece a context and a forum independent of her former US 'protector'. As Heinz Richter makes clear, Greece's main trouble at present is the Aegean and Cyprus conflict with Turkey which is the reason why she has so far been unable to get rid of the much-hated US bases, despite her parallel efforts to establish a Balkan nuclear-free zone.

Whilst it is obviously too early to speak of the history of post-Junta Greece, those who want the most recent background have a number of books to turn to. William Hardy McNeill's *The Metamorphosis of Greece wince World War II*, published in 1978, is a useful economic and sociological study based on developments in specific Greek villages and presenting a picture of social change. Roy C. Macridis' *Greek Politics at a Crossroads: What kind of Socialism?* would seem to echo Hoover Institute fears that Papandreou's Greece might escape from the Western sphere into Third World neutralism. More thorough studies of the PASOK (Papandreou) achievement will be found in two collections of papers. *Socialism in Greece*, edited by Dr. Zafiris Tzannatos gives a good account of the first stage of what George Catephores has defined as 'empirical socialism'. A more recent collection *Political Change in Greece: Before and after the Colonels*, edited by Kevin Featherstone and Dimitrios Katsoudas takes us from the end of the Civil War right up to the present day. Papers which appeared to the writer particularly useful are the Constitutional Analysis by D. Katsoudas, Vasilis Kapetanyannis on the Communists, Thanos Veremis on the Military and, in particular, Nicos Mouzelis' comparative study of the Venizelist and PASOK

144

movements which contributes to a real understanding of the latter. *Greece in the 1980s*, proceedings of a conference held at King's College in January 1981, edited by Richard Clogg, is angled towards future prospects as seen at the time. Two interesting, unusual papers are those by Peter Mackridge on Greek Culture and by Bishop Kallistos Ware on the Greek Church.

Epilogue

Readers who have had the patience to stay with this essay until now will, I hope, have formed some impression of what has happened in Greek historiography in the last 10 years. But it may be useful to conclude with a summary.

We have seen that Greece's Independence struggle of 1821–32 had left her, no longer an Ottoman province, but instead a protectorate of the European Powers, mainly of Britain. During the Second World War, a left-wing Resistance Movement, EAM–ELAS, with a membership of 1½ million active resisters out of a population of between 7 and 8 million and a moderate socialist programme – not unlike that of the British Labour Party of the period – tried to complete the unfinished business of 1821 and to achieve, not only liberation from Axis Occupation, but real independence. Their mistake was to imagine, first that their large membership would enable them to win power by constitutional means and secondly that the wartime Alliance would continue, and thus they failed both to appreciate the determination of British policy to re-impose its agent, an unpopular king addicted to unconstitutional rule; and to anticipate the Cold War, already at that time in preparation. A low-key reaction to what they were facing led to the clash of December 1944 and British armed intervention, setting in train the nightmare process of White Terror, Civil War and eventually the 7 years of Junta rule. This period was one of open client status for Greece, first under a British and then under a US 'protectorate'.

For most of these years any real attempt at assessment of the wartime Resistance would have been punishable by the courts as 'subversive propaganda'. The self-justificatory 'history' of the protecting powers: that their interventions were for the sake of saving Greece from a Communist take-

145

over by force of arms, was fostered by the client governments and prevailed in education and in the press.

Then, from the early '70s things began to change. First, the US and British official archives became accessible to researchers under the 25 and 30 Years Rules respectively and a very different picture began to emerge which has found its most cogent expression in the books of Papastratis, Richter and Wittner and also in a flood of conference papers and articles. Meanwhile, in 1974 the Junta fell, freedom of expression returned to Greece and the universities were reorganised and expanded with history established for the first time as an academic discipline and young foreign-trained post-graduates returning to teach; whilst, at the same time, a spate of protagonists' memoirs, long concealed in desk-drawers, was released into the bookshops. The final step came when the PASOK (Papandreou) Government officially recognised the EAM–ELAS Resistance and brought back the Civil War refugees from Eastern Europe. In Greece this radical shift found its academic expression in the First International Historians' Conference, held in Athens in April 1984, on the theme Dictatorship – Occupation – Resistance 1936–1944.

In the US there was at first some resistance to this shift and much talk of 'traditionalists' and 'revisionists'. But, partly because the US is a more open society than we have here and even more because Modern Greek History studies are largely in Greek–American hands, the change seems to have been more easily accepted, as it has been in Australia and Canada where the new books are in regular academic use and the only English edition of a Greek Resistance classic, Sarafis' *ELAS*, is a teaching text.

It is only in this country that the old official 'Chatham House' version of protectorate days is still fighting a rearguard action and this explains the vehemence of the backlash when the post-1970s version appeared in popular form in Jane Gabriel's 3-part television film, *Greece: The Hidden War*. No Greek will have been surprised at this and the writer herself, in an article in the Greek press in December 1984, had prophecised just such a backlash to the new version of wartime history. The TV film's crime was that what could be lived with as a debate between historians now appeared on the ordinary citizen's television screen, giving rise to such comments as 'But they never told us anything about all this' and thus enlightening the voting public about what may be done in its name.

In the writer's opinion it is time that we, in this country, come to terms with the results of recent documentary research, free ourselves from the papal infallibility of the 'Chatham House' version and relegate the stories of Britain saving Greece from a non-existent left-wing takeover and of ELAS 'marching on Athens' to the dustbin reserved for such colonial detritus.

NOTES

1. Shown by Channel 4 on 6th, 13th and 20th January 1986.
2. Here the writer follows the views of the late E. H. Carr, *What is History?*, Penguin Books, 1964, pp. 7–30; 119–32.
3. *For Freedom's Battle: Byron's Letters and Journals*, ed. Marchant, John Murrary, 1981, Vol. 11, p. 71.
4. *Otho I: King of Greece*, Leonard Bowen & Gordon Bolitho, London 1939, p. 106.
5. See Vol. II, p. 317.
6. A booklet with abstracts of the papers presented at this conference can be obtained on application to the writer.
7. Dr. Heinz Richter has suggested the following supplementary titles: Mario Cervi, *The Hollow Legions: Mussolini's Blunder in Greece 1940-1941*, Chatto & Windus, 1972; Robert Crisp, *The Gods were neutral*, Muller, 1960; Charles Cruickshank, *Greece 1940-1941*, David Pynter, 1976; Karl Gundelach, *The Battle for Crete 1941*, Deutsch, 1965; Toni Simpson, *Operation Mercury: the Battle of Crete 1941*, Hodder & Stoughton, 1982; Leland Stowe, *No other road to freedom*, New York, Faber & Faber, 1941; David Thomas, *Crete: The Battle at sea*, Deutsch, 1972.
8. In French: André Kedros, *La résistance grecque (1940-1944): Le combat d'un peuple pour la liberté*, Paris, Laffont, 1966 and now Christophe Chiclet, *Les Communistes grecs dans la Guerre*, Paris, L'Harmatton, 1987. In German: Heinz Richter, *Griechenland zwischen Revolution und Konterrevolution 1936-1946*, Frankfurt, Europäische Verlagsanstalt, 1973; and recently Hagen Fleischer, *Im Kreuzschatten der Mächte: Griechenland 1941-1944*, 2v. Frankfurt, Peter Lang Verlag, 1986.
9. 'EAM and the British Connection', in *Greece in the 1940s: A Nation in Crisis*, ed. John O. Iatrides, University Press of New England, 1981, pp. 81–101.
10. Lars Baerentzen, 'Anglo-German negotiations during the German retreat from Greece in 1944'. *Scandinavian Studies in Modern Greek*, 4 (1980), pp. 23–62; Heinz Richter, 'Lanz, Zervas and the British Liaison Officers', *The South Slav Journal*, 12, Nos. 43 and 4 (1989).
11. Christophe Chiclet, *Les Communistes grecs dans la Guerre*, Paris, L'Harmattan, 1987; Matthias Esche, *Die Kommunistische Partei Grechenlands 1941-1949*, Munchen, Wien, 1982; Antonio Solaro, *Storia del Partito Communista.Greco*, Milano, Teti Editore, 1974.
12. By Heinz Richter in *The South Slav Journal*, 5:4, Winter 1982-3, pp. 67–72.
13. Published in Athens in 1980 under the title *Meta ti Varkiza*.
14. Paris, Fayard, 1970.

15. As translator from the German, the writer must declare an interest here.
16. Sarafis himself warned Zachariadis that abstention would mean civil war.
17. *Greece: The Hidden War*, Channel 4, January 6th 1986.
18. *Studies in the History of the Greek Civil War 1945-1949*, ed. Lars Baerentzen, John O. Iatrides, Ole L. Smith, Copenhagen 1987.
19. In the Channel 4 Panel Debate programme on 3rd November 1986.
20. Foreign Office letter to T. George Thomas MP, RG10127 of 18.v.50 in League for Democracy in Greece archives at King's College, London.
21. Neal Ascherson in *The Observer*, 5.x.86.
22. *Les Forces Politiques en Grèce*, Montreal, 1965.
23. C. M. Woodhouse, *Something Ventured*, Granada, 1982, p. 195.
24. The Costas Gavras film 'Z' tells with considerable fidelity the story of a political assassination in 1963 which contributed to the fall of the Karamanlis Government.
25. The writer had direct personal experience of this. Required by her anti-Junta work to translate some of his speeches, she felt obliged to append a note to the effect that these incoherent utterances and misuse of everyday expressions (e.g. 'safety valve') were genuine. Later he was given a speech writer.

BIBLIOGRAPHY

(All books considered in the preceding essay are listed but listing does not necessarily imply recommendation.)

Alexander, George M, *The' Prelude to the Truman Doctrine: British Policy on Greece 1944-1947*. Oxford, Clarendon Press, 1982.
_____ 'The Demobilization Crisis of November 1944', in *Greece in the 1940s: A Nation in Crisis*, ed. John O. Iatrides, pp. 156-66.
Amnesty International, *Torture in Greece: The First Torturers' Trial 1975*, London, Amnesty International Pulications, 1977.
Andrews, Kevin, *The Flight of Ikaros: Travels in Greece during a civil war*, revised ed., Harmondsworth, Penguin, 1984.
_____ *Greece in the Dark 1967-1974*, Amsterdam, Hakkert, 1980.
Arnold, Percy, *Cyprus Challenge: A colonial island and its aspirations*, London, Hogarth Press, 1956.
Auty, Phyllia, ed., see Clogg, Richard.
Baerentzen, Lars, 'The Demonstration in Syntagma Square on Sunday 3rd December 1944', in *Scandinavian Studies in Modern Greek* 2 (1978), pp. 3-52.
_____ 'Anglo-German negotiations during the German retreat from Greece 1944', in *Ib.*, 4 (1980), pp. 23-62.
_____ (ed.), *British Reports on Greece 1943-1944*, Copenhagen, Museum Tusculaneum Press, 1982.
_____ (ed. with John Iatrides and Ole L. Smith), *Studies in the History of the Greek Civil War 1945-1949*, Copenhagen, Museum Tusculaneum Press, 1987.
Baillie-Grohman, H. T., see Heckstall-Smith, A.
Barker, Elisabeth, 'Greece in the Framework of Anglo-Soviet Relations 1941-1947', in *Greece: From Resistance to Civil War*, ed. M. Sarafis, pp. 15-27.
Barkman, Carl, *Ambassador in Athens*, London, Merlin Press, 1989.
Becket, James, *Barbarism in Greece*, New York, Walker, 1970.
Belli, Mihri, *Rigasin Dediği: What Rigas said*, 2nd ed., Stockholm, 1985.
Birtles, Bert, *Exiles in the Aegean: A personal narrative of Greek politics and travel*, London, Victor Gollancz, 1938.
Buckley, Christopher, *Greece and Crete 1941*, London, HMSO, 1952.
Byford-Jones, W., *The Greek Trilogy: Resistance, Liberation, Revolution*, London,

Hutchinson, N.D. (1945).

Capell, Richard, *Simiomata: A Greek Notebook 1944-1945*, London, McDonald, 1946.

Carey, A. and Carey, J., *The Web of Modern Greek Politics*, New York and London, Columbia University Press, 1968.

Chandler, Geoffrey, *The Divided Land: An Anglo-Greek Tragedy*, London, Macmillan, 1959.

Churchill, Winston, *The Second World War*, Harmondsworth, Penguin, 1985, Vol. III, pp. 83–97, 193–210; Vol. VI, pp. 92–103, 247–283.

Clive, Nigel, *A Greek Experience*, Michael Russell, 1985.

Clogg, Richard, *A Short History of Modern Greece*, Cambridge University Press, revised ed., 1985.

—— (ed. with George Yannopoulos), *Greece under Military Rule*, London, Secker & Warburg, 1972.

—— (ed. with Phyllis Auty), *British Policy towards Wartime Resistance in Yugoslavia and Greece*, London, Macmillan, 1975.

—— (ed.) *Greece in the 1980s*, London, Macmillan, 1983.

—— *Parties and Elections in Greece: The Search for Legitimacy*, London, C. Hurst and Co., 1988.

Cottrell, Richard, *Blood on their Hands: The Killing of Ann Chapman*, Grafton Books, 1987.

Couloumbis, Theodore *et al.* (ed.), *Foreign Interference in Greek Politics*, New York, Pella, 1976.

—— (ed. with John O. Iatrides), *Greek American Relations*, New York, Pella, 1980.

Couvaras, Costas, *OSS with the Central Committee of EAM*, San Francisco, Ware Press, 1982.

Deane, Philip (Tsigantes), *I should have died*, London, Hamish Hamilton, 1975.

EAM Central Committee, *White Book: May 1944-March 1945*, English ed., Greek–American Council, New York, 1945.

Eudes, Dominique, *The Kapitanios: Partisans and Civil War in Greece 1943-1949*, English ed., London, New Left Books, 1975.

Featherstone, Kevin (ed. with Dimitrios K. Katsoudas), *Political Change in Greece: Before and After the Colonels*, Croom Helm, 1987.

Fleischer, Hagen, 'The Anomalies in the Greek Middle East Forces 1941-1944', in *Journal of the Hellenic Diaspora*, V, 3 (1978), pp. 115–36.

Fleming, Amalia, *A Piece of Truth: Lady Fleming on the Colonels' Greece*, London, Cape, 1972.

Foley, Charles, *Island in Revolt*, London, Longmans, 1962.

—— (ed.), *The Memoirs of General Grivas*, London, Longmans, 1964.

Forster, E. S., *A Short History of Modern Greece 1821-1956*, revised 3rd ed., London, Methuen, 1958.

Fourtouni, Eleni, *Greek Women in Resistance*, New Haven, Thelphini Press, n.d.

Frangos, George, see Schwab, Peter.

Gage, Nicholas, *Eleni*, London, Collins, 1983.

Hammond, Nicholas, *Venture into Greece: With the guerillas 1943-1944*, London, Kimber, 1983.

Hamson, Denis, *We fell among Greeks: An autobiographical account of a military expedition to Greece in 1942*, London, Cape, 1946.

Haviaras, Stratis, *When the Tree Sings*, London, Pan Books, 1980.

—— *The Heroic Age*, London, Methuen, 1985.

(These are novels with an autobiographical background, a childhood during the Resistance years and a boyhood during the Civil War.)

Heckstall-Smith, A. and Baillie-Grohman, H. T., *Greek Tragedy 1941*, London, Blond, 1961.

Hitchens, Christopher, *Cyprus*, London, Quartet Books, 1984.
——— *The Elgin Marbles: Should they be returned to Greece?*, London, Chatto & Windus, 1987.
Holden, David, *Greece without columns: The Making of the Modern Greeks*, London, Faber, 1972.
Hondros, John Louis, *Occupation and Resistance: The Greek Agony 1941-1944*, New York, Pella, 1978.
Hourmouzios, S. L., *Starvation in Greece*, London, Harrison, 1943.
Iatrides, John O., *Revolt in Athens: The Greek Communist 'Second Round' 1944-1945*, Princeton University Press, 1972.
——— (ed.), *Ambassador MacVeagh Reports*, Princeton University Press, 1980.
——— (ed.), *Greece in the 1940s: A Nation in Crisis*, Hanover, University Press of New England, 1981.
——— 'Civil War 1945-1949', in *Greece in the 1940s*, ib., pp. 195-219.
——— (ed.), see Baerentzen, Lars.
——— (ed.), see Couloumbis, Theodore.
Jecchinis, Chris, *Beyond Olympus: The thrilling story of the train-busters in Nazi-occupied Greece*, London, Harrap, 1960.
Jordan, William, *Conquest without victory: A New Zealander's experiences in the Resistance Movements in Greece and France*, London, Hodder & Stoughton, 1969.
Katsoudas, Dimitrios K. (ed.), see Featherstone, Kevin.
Kofas, Jon V., *Authoritarianism in Greece' The Metaxas Regime*, New York, Columbia University Press, 1983.
——— *Intervention and Underdevelopment: Greece during the Cold War*, Pennsylvania State University Press, 1989 (an excerpt is included in this volume).
Koliopoulos, John S., *Greece and the British Connection 1935-1941*, Oxford, Clarendon Press, 1977.
Korovessis, Perikles, *The Method*, London, Allison & Busby, 1970.
Kousoulas, D. George, *Revolution and Defeat: The Story of the Greek Communist Party*, Oxford University Press, 1965.
Leeper, Reginald, *When Greek meets Greek*, London, Chatto & Windus, 1950.
Loulis, John C., *The Greek Communist Party 1940-1944*, Croom Helm, 1982.
McDonald, Robert, *Pillar and Tinderbox: The Greek Press and the Dictatorship*, London, Marion Boyars, 1982.
Mackenzie, Compton, *Wind of Freedom: The History of the Invasion of Greece by the Axis Powers 1940-1941*, London, Chatto & Windus, 1943.
——— *Greece in my life*, London, Chatto & Windus, 1960.
Macmillan, Harold, *The Blast of War 1939-1945*, London, Macmillan, 1967.
McNeill, William Hardy, *The Greek Dilemma: War and Aftermath*, London, Victor Gollancz, 1947.
——— *The Metamorphosis of Greece since World War II*, Oxford, Basil Blackwell, 1978.
Macridis, Roy C., *Greek Politics at a Cross-Roads: What kind of Socialism?*, Hoover Institution Press, 1984.
Matthews, Kenneth, *Memories of a Mountain War: Greece 1944-1949*, London, Longmans, 1972.
Maule, Henry, *Scobie, hero of Greece: the British campaign 1944-5*, London, Arthur Barker, 1978.
Moss, W. Stanley, *Ill met by Moonlight*, London, Harrap, 1950.
Mouzelis, Nicos P., *Modern Greece: Facets of Underdevelopment*, London, Macmillan, 1978.
Mulgan, John, *Report on Experience*, Oxford University Press, 1947.
Myers, E. C. W., *Greek Entanglement*, revised ed., Alan Sutton, 1985.
O'Ballance, Edgar, *The Greek Civil War 1944-1949*, London, Faber, 1966.

Panteli, Stavros, *A New History of Cyprus*, London, East-West Publications (UK) Ltd., 1984.

Papagos, Alexandros, *The Battle of Greece 1940-1941*, Athens, 1949.

Papandreou, Andreas, *Democracy at Gunpoint: The Greek Front*, Harmondsworth, Penguin, 1971.

Papandreou, George A., *The third war*, Athens, 1948.

Papandreou, Margaret, *Nightmare in Athens*, London, Prentice-Hall, 1970.

Papastratis, Procopis, *British policy towards Greece during the Second World War 1941-1944*, Cambridge University Press, 1984.

Psychoundakis, George, *The Cretan Runner: His story of the German Occupation*, London, Murray, 1978.

Richter, Heinz, *Greece and Cyprus since 1920: Bibliography of Contemporary History*, Nea Ellas Verlag, 1984 (11,500 titles). (This is a trilingual edition in English, German and Greek.)

—— *British Intervention in Greece: From Varkiza to Civil war*, English ed., London, Merlin Press, 1986.

—— 'Lanz, Zervas and the British Liaison Officers', in *The South Slav Journal*, 12, Nos. 43 and 4 (1989).

Roubatis, Yiannis P., *Tangled Webs: The US in Greece 1947-1967*, New York, Pella, 1987.

Rousseas, Stephen, *The Death of a Democracy*, New York, Grove Press, 1968.

Sarafis, Marion (ed.), *Greece: From Resistance to Civil War*, Nottingham, Spokesman, 1980.

Sarafis, Stefanos, *ELAS: Greek Resistance Army*, English ed., London, Merlin Press, 1980.

Schwab, Peter and George D. Frangos, *Greece under the Junta*, New York, Facts on File, 1970.

Smith, Ole L. (ed), see Baerentzen, Lars.

Stafford, David, *Britain and the European Resistance 1940-1945*, London, Macmillan, 1980.

Stavrianos, Leften S., *The Balkans since 1453*, New York, Rinehart & Co., 1958.

—— *Greece: American Dilemma and Opportunity*, Chicago, Regnery, 1952.

—— 'The Mutiny in the Greek Armed Forces April 1944', in *The American Slavic & East European Review* 9 (1950), pp. 302-11.

Stavrou, Nicholas A., *Allied Policy and Military Intervention: The Political role of the Greek military*, Athens, Papazisis, 1977.

Stephanides, Theodore, *Climax in Crete*, London, Faber, 1946.

Sweet-Escott, Bickham, *Greece: A political and economic survey 1939-1953*, Oxford University Press, 1954.

Theodoracopoulos, Taki, *The Greek Upheaveal*, Stacey International, 1976.

Theodorakis, Mikis, *Journals of Resistance*, English ed., London, Hart-Davis MacGibbon, 1973.

Tsoucalas, Constantine, *The Greek Tragedy*, English ed., Harmondsworth, Penguin, 1969.

Turner, Don, *Kiriakos: A British Partisan in Wartime Greece*, London, Robert Hale, 1982.

Tzannatos, Zafiris (ed.), *Socialism in Greece*, Aldershot, Gower, 1986.

Veremis, Thanos, *Greek Security Considerations: A Historical Perspective*, Athens, Papazisis, 1980.

Vlachos, Helen, *House Arrest*, London, Andre Deutsch, 1970.

Vlavianos, Haris, 'The Greek Communist Party in search of revolution', in Routledge's volume: *Resistance and Revolution and Mediterranean Europe*, ed. Tony Judt, London, 1989.

Vukmanović, Svetozar (General Tempo), *How and Why the People's Liberation Army of Greece met with Defeat*, English ed., Merlin Press, 1986.

Warner, Rex, *Men of Stones*, London, Bodley Head, 1949. (A novel, in the writer's opinion, based on Makronisos.)

Williamson, Hugh, *The Fourth Division*, London, Newman Neame, 1951.

Wittner, Lawrence S., *American Intervention in Greece 1943-1949*, New York, Columbia University Press, 1982.

Woodhouse, C. M., *Modern Greece: A Short History*, revised ed., London, Faber, 1985.

—— *Apple of Discord: A Survey of Recent Greek Politics in the international setting*, London, Hutchinson, 1948; re-issued Reston, Virginia, W.B. O'Neill, 1985.

—— *The Struggle for Greece 1941-1949*, London, Hart-Davis MacGibbon, 1976.

—— *Something Ventured*, London, Granada, 1982.

—— *Karamanlis: The Restorer of Greek Democracy*, Oxford, Clarendon Press, 1982.

—— *The Rise and Fall of the Greek Colonels*, London, Granada, 1982.

Wright, Colin, *British soldier in Greece*, Lawrence & Wishart, London, 1945.

Yannopoulos, George (ed.), see Clogg, Richard.

Zeï, Alki, *Wildcat under Glass*, English ed., London, Victor Gollancz, 1969. (A child's-eye view of the Metaxas regime.)

Selection of the most important works in French, German and Italian:

Chiclet, Christophe, *Les Communistes grecs dans la Guerre*, Paris, L'Harmattan, 1987.

Esche, Matthias, *Die Kommunistische Partei Griechenlands 1941-1949*, München, Wien, 1982.

Fleischer, Hagen, *Im Kreuzschatten der Mächte: Griechenland 1941-1944*, Frankfurt, 2 v. Peter Lang Verlag, 1986.

Kedros, André, *La résistance grecque 1940-1944: Le combat d'un peuple pour la liberté*, Paris, Laffont, 1966.

Richter, Heinz, *Griechenland zwischen Revolution und Konterrevolution 1936-1946*, Frankfurt, Europäische Verlagsanstalt, 1973.

—— *Friede in der Ägäis? Zypern-Ägäis – Minderheiten*, Köln, Romiosini, 1989.

Solaro, Antonio, *Storia del Partito Communista Greco*, Milane, Teti Editore, 1974.

ADDENDUM

As this goes to press here is a new book, on the history, customs and literature of Crete. *Under Mount Ida: a Journey into Crete* by Oliver Burch (Ashford, 1989) is pleasantly written and attractively presented. For the writer of this essay who did three seasons' archaeological work in Crete pre-war, it seems essential and accessible reading for the visitor who wants to go beyond the guide-books, and can be thoroughly recommended on all matters concerning Crete.